VOCABULARY

Meaning and Message

Number 3

Stella Sands

Fearon/Janus
Belmont, California

Simon & Schuster Supplementary Education Group

CONTENTS

ISBN 0-8224-9478-7

Printed in the United States of America.   2. 10 9 8 7 6 5 4 3 2
BA

Cover Illustrator: Hank Osuna
Cover Designer: Dianne Platner
Illustrators: James Balkovek, James McConnell,
Margaret Sanfilippo

Reading on Your Own

Name _____ Date _____

As you read this story, think about the meaning of each highlighted word.

Fire Drill

It was fire safety day in Kelly's class. Members of the local fire department were coming to teach the class what to do in a fire.

Captain Davis was the first officer to speak. He told the students that there is a **correct** way and an incorrect way to **leave** a room in case of a fire. "The first thing to remember is to stay calm," said Captain Davis. "If everyone tries to leave at once, someone will get hurt." Kelly and her friends already knew this from the fire drills they had taken part in every month.

Captain Davis then told them a few **details** about fire safety that they hadn't heard before. "If you are in a building that has an elevator," he said, "don't use it if there's a fire. Look for a **sign** that says 'Exit.' This will lead you to the stairs. Also, if there is smoke in the hall, crawl along the floor to find the exit. The closer you are to the floor, the more fresh air there is." Kelly learned that more people die from breathing in smoke than from being burned by flames.

Captain Davis offered another safety tip. "If you are in a room in a burning building," he said, "feel the door. If the door is hot, that means **danger.** The fire is too **close.** Try to leave through a window. If the window is too high, wait for help."

Kelly and her classmates were also given a short lesson in **first aid.** They learned how to treat minor burns. They were taught what to do if a person passes out from too much smoke.

Before leaving, the fire officers checked the condition of the **fire escape** on the side of the building. Those steel stairs are another way for people to leave a building in case of a fire. There was also a short fire drill. Everyone calmly left the building and gathered outside near the **entrance** to the schoolyard.

Kelly had enjoyed fire safety day. She also felt a lot safer now.

If you woke up in the middle of the night and your home was on fire, what would be your plan for escape?

_____

_____

_____

Using Context

Name _____ Date _____

Choose a word from the box that means the same as the highlighted word or words in each sentence below.

close	correct	danger	details	entrance
exit	fire escape	first aid	leave	sign

1. Janine is very good in math. All her answers on the last test were **without mistakes.** _____

2. It takes me only one minute to walk to Eleanor's house. She lives **near** to me. _____

3. Petra had to walk around the block to find the **place to go into** to the theater. _____

4. After the movie, everyone left through the **way out.**

   _____

5. "Open at noon," said the **notice with information on it** in the store window. _____

6. The library closes at 6:00. Everyone must **go away from** the building by then. _____

7. Sara told me all the **parts that made up** of the plan.

   _____

8. When the child ran into the street, he was in **chance of harm.**

   _____

9. When Simone burned her hand, her mother gave her **treatment before a doctor can come.** _____

10. The family fled the smoke and flames by going down the **metal stairs outside the building.** _____

Vocabulary Development: Multiple Meanings

Name _____ Date _____

Do you know the meanings of the words in italics in the sentences below?

The *patient* was *patient* as she waited for her operation to begin.
I was eating a *mint* while working in the *mint*.
Don't *rest* when the *rest* of the class is busy working.

You probably noticed that the same word appears twice in each sentence. You probably also noticed that the italicized words in each sentence have different meanings. In the first sentence, the word *patient* means "a person who is under the care of a doctor." It also means "showing the ability not to get upset too quickly." In the second sentence, the word *mint* means both "a candy" and "a place where money is made." In the third sentence, *rest* means both "to relax" and "that which is left" or "the others."

As you can see, one word can be used as more than one part of speech. In the first sentence, *patient* is used as both a noun and an adjective. In the third sentence, *rest* is used as a verb *and* a noun.

Many words in the English language are like this. It makes sense to study these words. By knowing their different meanings, you will be better able to understand what you read and hear. You will also be better prepared to speak and write clearly.

As your language skills develop, so will your ability to understand and live in your world. When you can express yourself clearly, you can make your life better. You will have more power.

Each highlighted word below can be used in more than one way. Look up the words in a dictionary or the glossary at the back of this book. Write two definitions for each word. Then use each word in a sentence of your own that shows you understand its meaning.

1. **close**

First definition: _____

Sentence: _____

_____

Second definition: _____

Sentence: _____

_____

Vocabulary Development: Multiple Meanings

Name _____ Date _____

2. correct

First definition: _____

Sentence: _____

_____

Second definition: _____

Sentence: _____

_____

3. entrance

First definition: _____

Sentence: _____

_____

Second definition: _____

Sentence: _____

_____

4. leave

First definition: _____

Sentence: _____

_____

Second definition: _____

Sentence: _____

_____

5. sign

First definition: _____

Sentence: _____

_____

Second definition: _____

Sentence: _____

_____

Puzzle

Name _____ Date _____

A. Choose the word from the box to complete each sentence below. Write one letter in each blank.

danger	details	first aid	close	entrance
exit	sign	leave	correct	fire escape

1. free of error __ __ __ __ __ __ __

　　　　　　　1　　　13

2. items; small parts that make up something

__ __ __ __ __ __ __

　　　　　3

3. depart __ __ __ · __ __

　　　　4　　　　10

4. not far __ __ __ __ __

　　　　　　　16

5. metal stairs outside a building

__ __ __ __ __ __ __ __ __ __

5　6　　　　　　　11

6. billboard __ __ __ __

　　　　　17

7. possibility of something bad happening __ __ __ __ __ __

　　　　　　　　　　　　　　12

8. the way into something __ __ __ __ __ __ __ __ .

　　　　　　　　　　2　　　8

9. the way out of something __ __ __ __

　　　　　　　　　14

10. emergency medical care __ __ __ __ __ __ __

　　　　　　　7　　18　　　9

B. To solve this puzzle, write each numbered letter above in the matching blank below. The letters will spell something you should do in case of fire.

__ __ __ __ __ __ __ __

1　2　3　4　5　6　7　8

__ __ __ __ __ __ __*m*__ __ __

9　10　11　12　13　14　15　16　17　18

Vocabulary: Meaning and Message © Fearon/Janus Publishers

Dictionary Skills: Meet the Dictionary

Name _____ Date _____

A dictionary is one of the most useful books there is. For instance, it can tell you what the word *abolish* means and how it is pronounced. A dictionary can tell you where the word *convention* comes from and what part of speech it is. It can tell you when Abraham Lincoln was president and when he died. A dictionary can tell you that *lend an ear* does not mean "to give someone your ear for a short time." It can tell you the difference between the words *desert* and *dessert*. It can tell you if a word has any synonyms or antonyms. Almost anything you want to know about a word can be found in a dictionary.

Here is a dictionary entry for the word *event*. The labels show the kind of information being offered.

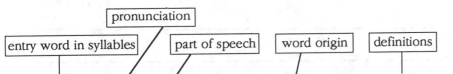

| pronunciation |
| entry word in syllables | part of speech | word origin | definitions |

e vent (i vent′) **noun** [from Latin *eventus,* event] **1.** something that takes place; usually, something important **2.** a contest in a sports program—*SYN.* see OCCURRENCE—**in any event** anyhow; in any case

| synonym | idiom |

Become familiar with your dictionary. Keep it handy when you read. Make a habit of looking up words you're not sure of. If you do, your power of speech and your understanding will increase greatly.

Write *yes* beside each question whose answer you can find in a dictionary. Write *no* beside each question whose answer you cannot find in a dictionary.

1. _____ How is the word *Australia* pronounced?

2. _____ What do I do if I get caught in a burning building?

3. _____ How is the word *flammable* divided into syllables?

4. _____ What is the meaning of the word *flammable*?

5. _____ Does the word *safety* come from a foreign language?

6. _____ What is the opposite (antonym) of the word *exit*?

7. _____ When did the last large forest fire take place in my state?

Writing on Your Own

Name _____ Date _____

Suppose a house two blocks away from your house is on fire.
You decide to leave your house immediately. On your way out,
you pick up a few of your favorite items. What five items
would you take with you? Tell why you would take each one.

_____

_____

_____

_____

_____

_____

_____

Luckily, the fire was stopped by the fire department before it
got to your house. Firefighters risk their own lives trying to
save other people's lives. So do police officers and the
members of rescue teams. Would you like to have a job in
which you try to save others' lives? Tell why or why not.

_____

_____

_____

_____

_____

_____

_____

Vocabulary: Meaning and Message © Fearon/Janus Publishers

Test

Name _____ Date _____

Choose the best word to complete each sentence. Write the letter on the line.

1. The puppy stayed _____ to her new owner.

   A. entrance   B. exit   C. sign   D. close

2. I usually add too much salt when I make soup. This time, however, I added the _____ amount.

   A. sign   B. correct   C. close   D. details

3. You can go in by the _____ door on your left.

   A. details   B. entrance   C. fire escape   D. exit

4. A fallen tree blocked our _____ from the park.

   A. entrance   B. exit   C. sign   D. danger

5. I found my way by reading the _____.

   A. sign   B. entrance   C. exit   D. detail

6. When summer vacation begins, we will _____ for a trip to New England.

   A. leave   B. sign   C. entrance   D. correct

7. The firefighters carried six people down the _____ .

   A. first aid   B. sign   C. fire escape   D. details

8. Many day-care workers take courses in _____ . They must know what to do if a child gets hurt.

   A. correct   B. signs   C. details   D. first aid

9. As the fire spread, we were in _____ of losing our home.

   A. details   B. signs   C. danger   D. entrances

10. I have an idea of what I want to do, but I haven't worked out all the _____ yet.

    A. first aid   B. details   C. correction   D. sign

Reading on Your Own

Name _____ Date _____

As you read this story, think about the meaning of each highlighted word.

Dining Out

Joni's parents were taking her and her brother Sam to a new **restaurant.** The restaurant served Italian food. Joni had been looking forward all day to a great meal.

Sam was only four years old. As soon as everyone sat down in the restaurant, he took his napkin and put it on his head. Then he started singing at the top of his lungs. Joni's father told him to stop. "That is not the **appropriate** way to act," he said. "This is a **public** place. We're not at home." Sam knew that his father was giving him a **warning.** He would have to behave.

The waiter brought menus to the table. Joni was told she could have soup or a salad to begin her meal. She chose a green salad with Italian dressing. For her main course, she asked for spaghetti with tomato sauce. Sam wanted pizza with everything on it.

Before the food arrived, Joni's mother reminded Joni to wash her hands. Joni asked the waiter where the **restrooms** were. He pointed to the back of the restaurant. At first, Joni got lost. She walked through a door marked **"private"** and into the kitchen. A cook told her she had gone in the wrong door.

Soon Joni found two other doors. The first was marked **"Ladies."** The second was marked **"Gentlemen."** The second door, however, had a sign on it that said **"Out of Order."** Happy that the ladies' room was working, Joni walked in and washed her hands.

Then Joni returned to the table, where the food was waiting. The meal was delicious. Sam loved his pizza. Joni loved her spaghetti. After everyone had eaten, Joni's father paid the bill and left a tip for the waiter.

As they left, Sam spotted a dish of candy on a **shelf** near the door. He reached up to take a piece and brought the whole dish crashing to the floor. Sam was upset, but everyone in the restaurant laughed. Even Joni's father had to smile.

Do you like eating in a restaurant? Why or why not?

_____

_____

_____

Vocabulary: Meaning and Message © Fearon/Janus Publishers

Lesson 2, Exercise 2
Using Context

Name _____ Date _____

Circle the word that fits the definition.

1. suitable for the purpose; correct; proper

   public   private   appropriate

2. a kind and polite man

   private   gentleman   restaurant

3. not working

   out of order   warning   private

4. belonging to a particular person or group, not to everyone

   public   private   appropriate

5. a place in which food is prepared and served

   restroom   public   restaurant

6. a room in a public building having a sink and a toilet

   restroom   private   appropriate

7. a notice of danger

   appropriate   shelf   warning

8. having to do with the people as a whole; for use by everyone

   public   private   restaurant

9. a woman who is polite and well-mannered

   lady   gentleman   appropriate

10. a piece of wood or other material that is used to hold things. It is often hung from a wall.

   restaurant   restroom   shelf

Vocabulary Development: Plural Nouns

Name _____ Date _____

You know that a **singular noun** is a word that names one person, place, or thing. A word that names more than one person, place, or thing is a **plural noun.** Plural nouns are formed from singular nouns in several different ways. Here are some rules to help you form plural nouns correctly.

Rule 1: It's easy to make most singular nouns plural. Simply add *s* to the singular noun.

Singular nouns:	car	restaurant	room	warning
Plural nouns:	cars	restaurants	rooms	warnings

Rule 2: To form the plural of a noun ending in *ch, sh, s, x,* or *z,* add *es.*

Singular nouns:	bench	dish	gas	fox	buzz
Plural nouns:	benches	dishes	gases	foxes	buzzes

Rule 3: To form the plural of a noun ending in a vowel and a *y,* add *s.* (The vowels are *a, e, i, o,* and *u.*)

Singular nouns:	monkey	donkey	tray	toy
Plural nouns:	monkeys	donkeys	trays	toys

Rule 4: To form the plural of a noun ending in a consonant and a *y,* change the *y* to *i* and add *es.* (A consonant is any letter other than *a, e, i, o,* or *u.*)

Singular nouns:	pony	lady	library	candy
Plural nouns:	ponies	ladies	libraries	candies

Rule 5: To form the plural of nouns ending in *o,* check your dictionary. Some of these plurals are formed by adding *es* to the singular nouns. Others are formed simply by adding *s.*

Singular nouns:	hero	tomato	piano	radio
Plural nouns:	heroes	tomatoes	pianos	radios

Rule 6: To form the plural of a word ending in *f* or *fe,* check your dictionary. The plurals of some of these nouns are formed by changing the *f* or *fe* to *ve* and adding *s.* The plurals of others are formed by adding *s.*

Singular nouns:	shelf	thief	roof	safe
Plural nouns:	shelves	thieves	roofs	safes

Vocabulary Development: Plural Nouns

Nasme_____ Date _____

Rule 7: Some nouns that name animals have the same singular and plural forms.

Singular nouns: deer   moose   sheep   salmon
Plural nouns: deer   moose   sheep   salmon

Rule 8: Some nouns are "irregular." The best way to know how to make them plural is to memorize the plural forms.

Singular nouns: gentleman   child   ox   woman
Plural nouns: gentlemen   children   oxen   women

Follow the rules to change each highlighted noun from singular to plural. Rewrite each sentence.

1. **Rule 1.** Put the **spoon** on the **plate.**

   _____

2. **Rule 2.** The **fox** hid in the **bush.**

   _____

3. **Rule 3.** Give the **key** to the **boy.**

   _____

4. **Rule 4.** We bought clothes for the **baby.**

   _____

5. **Rule 5.** Turn on your **radio.**

   _____

6. **Rule 6.** The police caught the **thief.**

   _____

7. **Rule 7.** The **deer** escaped the hunters.

   _____

8. **Rule 8.** The **man** and the **woman** went to the park.

   _____

Puzzle

Name _____ Date _____

Use the clues to help you complete the crossword puzzle. The answers can be found in the box.

> appropriate   gentleman   lady   order   shelf
> restroom   restaurant   public   warning   private

Across
3. fitting; well-suited; proper
5. the opposite of *private*
7. a small platform attached to a wall
9. a bathroom
10. "Watch out!"

Down
1. a polite woman
2. a polite man
4. the opposite of *public*
6. a place where food is served
8. Something that doesn't work is *out of* _____.

Dictionary Skills: Alphabetizing

Name _____ Date _____

We often read things that are arranged in alphabetical order. For instance, names in a telephone book are arranged in alphabetical order. Last names beginning with the letter *A* come first. These are followed by last names beginning with *B*, then *C*, and so on.

The items in dictionaries and encyclopedias are also arranged in alphabetical order. A list of the students in your class would probably be arranged alphabetically.

When things are arranged in alphabetical order, it is easier for us to find them. If we're looking at a list for a name beginning with the letter *Y*, we know to look toward the bottom of the list. If we're looking for a name beginning with the letter *D*, we know to look toward the top of the list.

When words begin with the same first letter, we use the second letter to decide the alphabetical order of the words. When words begin with the same first two letters, we use the third letter to decide the order, and so on. Here are some examples of words in alphabetical order. In each case, the highlighted letter determines the order of the words.

Words beginning with the same first letter:

aim   alarm   any   ape

Aim comes before *alarm* because *i* comes before *l*. *Alarm* comes before *any* because *l* comes before *n*. *Any* comes before *ape* because *n* comes before *p*.

Words beginning with the same first two letters:

draw   dress   drink   drum

Words beginning with the same first three letters:

trade   traffic   trail   trap

Imagine yourself working in a restaurant. You have to make sure that there's always enough food on hand to serve the customers. When there isn't, you must order more. Below is a list of food items you might need to buy. Arrange the list in alphabetical order. Write *1* next to the first item, *2* next to the second item, and so on.

_____ soup   _____ sardines   _____ bacon   _____ meat

_____ juice   _____ grapes   _____ butter   _____ soda

_____ jelly   _____ milk   _____ bread   _____ grapefruit

Writing on Your Own

Name _____ Date _____

People called *critics* review such things as books, movies, and restaurants. Their reviews appear in newspapers and magazines. The reviews help readers decide if they will see the movie, for instance, or go to the restaurant.

Suppose you are a restaurant critic. It's up to you to write a short review of a restaurant in your town. First, choose a restaurant to review. It can be a diner, a pizza shop, or a hot dog stand. The restaurant can be a real place or one that you have made up. Write the name of your restaurant here.

_____

Now decide what you want to say about the restaurant. You could discuss the food, the service, the prices, and what the restaurant looks like. You might want to say which dishes you like and which you don't like and tell why. You could compare this restaurant to another one. Jot down whatever ideas you have about your restaurant. For instance, you might write, "Tony's onion rings cost more than anyone else's, but they're worth it." Then tell why you think Tony's onion rings are so good. Begin on the lines below. If you need more room, use a separate sheet of paper.

_____

_____

_____

_____

_____

_____

_____

When you finish, organize your ideas into a short review of the restaurant. You and your classmates may want to read your reviews aloud to one another. See if you have any different opinions about the same places.

Vocabulary: Meaning and Message © Fearon/Janus Publishers

Test

Name _____ Date _____

Choose the best word to complete each sentence.

1. "Smoking can ruin your health," are words of _____.

   A. public   B. private   C. appropriate   D. warning

2. Today I ate lunch in a _____.

   A. restaurant   B. warning   C. public   D. appropriate

3. When going to a job interview, wear _____ clothing.

   A. warning   B. out of order   C. private   D. appropriate

4. Do you know where I can find the _____ in this building?

   A. restroom   B. order   C. shelf   D. public

5. Books about cars are on the top _____ of the bookcase.

   A. public   B. shelf   C. restroom   D. appropriate

6. We can't use the soda machine. It's _____.

   A. out of order   B. warn   C. appropriate   D. restroom

7. This is between you and me. It's a _____ matter.

   A. private   B. warn   C. appropriate   D. gentleman

8. Everyone was invited to the _____ meeting.

   A. public   B. warning   C. shelf   D. restaurant

9. Fancy dresses can be found in the _____ formalwear department.

   A. restaurant   B. ladies'   C. public   D. appropriate

10. Leroy is trustworthy, kind, and well mannered. He's a real _____.

    A. gentleman   B. private   C. warning   D. shelf

Reading on Your Own

Name _____ Date _____

As you read this story, think about the meaning of each highlighted word.

A Move to the City

The Brody family was moving to the **city.** They had been living for years in the country. Now both Mr. and Mrs. Brody were changing jobs. It would be better for them to live closer to their work.

Moving to the city meant that they would be leaving their house and living in an **apartment** building. They would pay **rent** every month to live in one of the apartments.

On Sunday, the Brodys looked at the **real estate** listings in the newspaper. The "Apartments for Rent" section took up a whole page. The Brodys circled ads for several apartments that seemed to be what they were looking for. They called the people renting out the apartments and made appointments to see them.

That Friday, they began their search. The **owner** of one building seemed very nice. Then he learned that the Brodys had two children and a dog. Suddenly he no longer seemed so friendly. "Kids and animals will destroy my **property**!" he screamed. The Brodys left.

They visited seven apartment buildings. By the time they reached the last one, they were very tired. Mr. Brody was ready to give up. Mrs. Brody begged him to look at one more apartment.

When they saw it, they discovered it was exactly what they had been looking for. There were two bedrooms, a large kitchen, a bathroom, and a living room. The price was right and the **landlord,** Mrs. Best, loved children and pets! "I've owned this building for twenty-five years," she said. "I always know who will be good **tenants.** You'll be perfect!"

Mrs. Best then introduced the Brodys to Joe, the building **superintendent.** "Joe keeps the building in perfect order," said Mrs. Best. The Brodys could hardly wait to sign the **lease.** This piece of paper was a legal agreement between the Brodys and Mrs. Best. The Brodys agreed to rent the apartment for two years.

"Welcome to the city!" said Mrs. Best as the Brodys signed their names on the lease.

Would you prefer to live in a house or an apartment? Why?

_____

_____

_____

Vocabulary: Meaning and Message © Fearon/Janus Publishers

Using Context

Name _____ Date _____

Circle the word that best completes each sentence.

1. In some cities, most people live in _____.

   owners   apartments   landlords   tenants

2. Edgar put a fence around his _____.

   property   tenant   landlord   lease

3. Georgia signed a one-year _____ on a new apartment.

   tenant   property   lease   superintendent

4. Myra asked the _____ to fix the sink in her apartment.

   lease   apartment   tenant   superintendent

5. We don't own the house we live in. We _____ it.

   landlord   rent   property   tenant

6. Antonio is the proud _____ of a new car.

   landlord   superintendent   tenant   owner

7. The buildings on this block are all owned by one _____.

   landlord   apartment   lease   property

8. Rudy pays $300.00 a month to be a _____ in Mrs. Jason's apartment building.

   landlord   tenant   superintendent   lease

9. We live in the country, outside _____ limits.

   city   landlord   apartment   tenant

10. It costs a lot to buy a house there. The _____ prices are high.

   rent   lease   real estate   tenant

Vocabulary Development: Possessives

Name _____ Date _____

If you possess something, you own it. To show that we own cars, appliances, or pets, we sometimes use ownership papers, registration cards, and licenses. When we're writing, we don't need all these pieces of paper to show possession. All we need are apostrophes and the letter *s*.

The information below will show you how to make singular and plural nouns possessive.

To make most singular nouns possessive, add *'s* to the noun.

Singular nouns	Singular possessive nouns
Mary	Mary's real estate
catcher	catcher's mitt
book	book's jacket

To make singular nouns that end in *s* or *z* possessive, add *'s*. However, if this makes it awkward to say the word, add only an apostrophe.

Singular nouns	Singular possessive nouns
James	James's peach
boss	boss's desk
Dickens	Dickens' novels

To make a plural noun ending in *s* possessive, add only an apostrophe.

Plural nouns	Plural possessive nouns
girls	girls' hats
dogs	dogs' leashes
parents	parents' cars

Treat plural nouns that do not end in *s* as if they were singular nouns. Simply add *'s* to make them possessive.

Plural nouns	Plural possessive nouns
women	women's coats
sheep	sheep's wool
children	children's playground

Certain pronouns can also be used to show ownership. Apostrophes are not used with them. They include **my, mine, your, yours, his, her, hers, its, our, ours, their,** and **theirs.**

This apartment is mine.
That apartment is yours.
Their apartments are quite large.

Vocabulary: Meaning and Message © Fearon/Janus Publishers

Vocabulary Development: Possessives

Name _____ Date _____

A. The *singular* possessive noun in each sentence below is spelled incorrectly. Rewrite the sentence with the noun spelled correctly.

1. We found a **horses'** hoofprints on our property.

_____

2. That **foxs** paw is bleeding.

_____

3. The **superintendents'** tools are missing.

_____

4. One **students** jacket was torn.

_____

5. The **citys'** mayor was reelected.

_____

6. My **childs** room is a mess.

_____

B. The *plural* possessive noun in each sentence below is spelled incorrectly. Rewrite the sentence with the noun spelled correctly.

1. The three **animal's** owners were feeding them.

_____

2. The landlord listened to the **tenants's** complaints.

_____

3. Those **sheeps** wool will make many warm coats.

_____

4. The two **citie's** police departments often work together.

_____

5. The property on the hillside is **theirs'**.

_____

Puzzle

Name _____ Date _____

A. **The words in the box can be found in the puzzle below. They may be written in any direction. Find and circle each one. You may want to check off each word in the box after you have circled it. One word has been circled and checked as an example.**

apartment	city	landlord	lease	✔owner
real estate	tenant	property	rent	superintendent

```
e r e a l e s t a t e s d c
o l a n p p l e a s e e m
d w w e l r c a c a t m p j
s r n p c o t n h i c y g i
w r v e h p g d i y t t q g
h e n g r e c l m i n e w f
x n y q a r z o c h h n p n
s t g h n t z r m o i a h t
v f h n m y l d j o g n z c
d e c a p a r t m e n t e r
s r e p l d r o c u o p p p
s u p e r i n t e n d e n t
```

B. **Choose any three words from the box. Use each one in a sentence of your own.**

1. _____

_____

2. _____

_____

3. _____

_____

Vocabulary: Meaning and Message © Fearon/Janus Publishers

Dictionary Skills: Guide Words

Name _____ Date _____

Here are three questions to think about: Can guide words be found at the bottom of each dictionary page? Can guide words help you find words in a dictionary quickly? Could the guide words for *peach* be **banana** and **grape?**

The answer to the first question is *no*. Guide words are found on the top of each dictionary page. The word on the left tells you the first word defined on that page. The word on the right tells you the last word defined on that page.

The answer to the second question is *yes*. The words that come alphabetically between the guide words on any page will be defined on that dictionary page.

The answer to the third question is *no. Peach* does not come alphabetically between *banana* and *grape*. The guide words for *peach* could be **peace** and **pear,** for instance. *Peach* comes alphabetically between those two words.

A. Read each set of guide words. Write one word that could appear on a dictionary page containing those guide words. Use your dictionary for help.

1. city/clam   _____

2. apartment/appeal   _____

3. property/protect   _____

4. lease/ledge   _____

B. Circle the words that could be found on the same page as the guide words.

1. **textbook/thermometer**

   that   theme   telescope   tap

   there   theater   this   test

2. **stand/state**

   star   starve   stampede   stalk

   staple   steel   statue   stare

Writing on Your Own

Name _____ Date _____

Imagine that you are a working adult. You live in a city where you enjoy your job and have many friends. One close friend is thinking about leaving the city and moving to the country. You don't want your friend to do this.

First, imagine why your friend might want to make this decision. Write down five reasons he or she might have for moving. Number each reason as you write it.

_____

_____

_____

_____

Now write your response to each of those reasons. Number your responses to correspond to the reasons.

_____

_____

_____

_____

_____

_____

_____

Finally, on a separate sheet of paper, write a letter to convince your friend to stay in the city. Be polite, but tell your friend how you feel and make a strong argument for your point of view. Be as clear and convincing as you can when responding to your friend's reasons for moving.

Vocabulary: Meaning and Message © Fearon/Janus Publishers

Test

Name _____ Date _____

Choose the best word or phrase to fit each definition.

1. a room or group of rooms in which one can live

   A. real estate   B. apartment   C. landlord   D. city

2. payment for the use of something, such as an apartment

   A. rent   B. tenant   C. landlord   D. property

3. a place where people live and work that is larger than a town

   A. real estate   B. property   C. city   D. apartment

4. the person to whom something belongs

   A. renter   B. superintendent   C. tenant   D. owner

5. that which a person or group owns

   A. tenant   B. property   C. superintendent   D. rent

6. a written rental agreement

   A. rent   B. property   C. landlord   D. lease

7. a person who keeps a building clean and in shape; a person who is in charge

   A. superintendent   B. tenant   C. renter   D. apartment

8. the owner of buildings that are rented

   A. superintendent   B. landlord   C. renter   D. tenant

9. buildings and the land they are on

   A. real estate   B. apartments   C. leases   D. tenants

10. a person who pays in order to live in a rented house or apartment

    A. landlord   B. property   C. tenant   D. owner

Vocabulary: Meaning and Message © Fearon/Janus Publishers

Reading on Your Own

Name _____ Date _____

As you read this story, think about the meaning of each highlighted word.

Who's Calling?

Knowing a few tips on how to use a telephone can save you time and money. It may even save someone's life.

The first thing to know is what to do in case of an **emergency.** If there's danger and you need some help, use the phone right away. In most places, you can call the same number for **police,** fire, and ambulance service. Usually that number is 911. If your area doesn't have 911 service, call whichever service you need. You can also call the **operator.** Dial 0 and say, "This is an emergency." Then tell the operator what is happening and where. The operator will call whichever emergency service you need.

It's a good idea to list emergency numbers next to the phone. You can find them in the front of the phone book, or **directory.**

Of course we don't use the phone only to handle emergencies. We also use it simply to stay in touch with friends. Calling someone who lives far away can be a lot of fun. Long **distance** calls can also cost a lot of money. However, there are ways to save money. For example, you can dial directly, without asking the operator for **assistance.** To do this, first dial your friend's **area code.** These three numbers show which part of the country you are calling.

You can get **discounts** on the costs of your calls by phoning in the evening, at night, and on weekends. The operator can tell you how much it will cost per minute to call any number at any time.

At some point, you may have to ask the person you are calling to pay for the call. The operator will connect you if the other person is willing to accept the charges. If that person does not want to pay for a **collect** call, the operator will **cancel** the call. No one will be charged. To call collect, dial 0, then area code, then number.

If you don't know someone's area code or phone number, look in the phone book or dial information at 411.

The telephone can be a wonderful means of communication. It makes sense to learn to use it wisely.

If you could call anyone in the world, who would it be? Why?

_____

_____

_____

Vocabulary: Meaning and Message © Fearon/Janus Publishers

Lesson 4, Exercise 2
Using Context

Name _____ Date _____

Circle the word that fits the definition.

1. three numbers that are dialed when calling a non-local phone number

   collect   area code   operator

2. the kind of phone call paid for by the person who answers

   long distance   cancel   collect

3. something that happens without warning and that demands action

   collect   assistance   emergency

4. a listing of names, addresses, and telephone numbers; a telephone book

   directory   assistance   collect

5. help; aid

   police   directory   assistance

6. money subtracted from the price of something

   assistance   discount   collect

7. the space between two places; a faraway place

   distance   operator   discount

8. a group of people who keep law and order

   emergency   operators   police

9. to call off; to withdraw; to say that something will be no more

   operator   area code   cancel

10. a person who helps people place telephone calls and provides information about the phone system

    discount   operator   police

Vocabulary: Meaning and Message © Fearon/Janus Publishers

Vocabulary Development: Compounds

Name _____ Date _____

Compound words, or compounds, are words that are made up of two or more smaller words. Often you can figure out what a compound means by thinking about the parts of the larger word. For instance, let's say you read this sentence:

The countdown was about to begin.

If you don't know the meaning of *countdown,* look at the words that make it up, *count* and *down.* Think about the meanings of these two words. You might come up with the definition of *countdown* as "a counting of time backwards." A countdown is just that. It tells how much time is left before something takes place.

Some compounds, such as *countdown,* are written as one word. Some are written as separate words. Some have hyphens(-) between their word parts. Here are examples of the three types of compound words:

One word	Separate words	Words with hyphens
homeland	key ring	father-in-law
necktie	half brother	editor-in-chief
halfway	landing field	forget-me-not

A. Try to guess the meanings of these compounds by studying their parts. Write a short definition for each. Then look up the compound in a dictionary. If you guessed incorrectly, write the correct definition. Then use each word in a sentence of your own.

1. **fireplace** _____

_____

_____

_____

2. **bookmark** _____

_____

_____

_____

Vocabulary: Meaning and Message © Fearon/Janus Publishers

Vocabulary Development: Compounds

Name _____ Date _____

3. **self-portrait**

_____

_____

_____

4. **rain forest**

_____

_____

_____

B. The compound words below appeared in the story on page 28. Use each one in a sentence of your own.

1. **area code** _____

_____

_____

2. **collect call** _____

_____

_____

3. **phone book** _____

_____

_____

4. **weekend** _____

_____

_____

5. **long distance** _____

_____

_____

Vocabulary: Meaning and Message © Fearon/Janus Publishers

Puzzle

Name _____ Date _____

Unscramble the highlighted letters to form a word that makes sense in each sentence below. The words are in the box. Write the words on the lines.

> area code   operator   assistance   police   discount
> directory   cancel   collect   distance   emergency

1. I saw a bright light in the far **s t n c a e d i.**

   _____

2. Everything is being sold at 30% **o u d i n t s c.**

   _____

3. I have no money and must call **l l c o e t c.**

   _____

4. When calling long distance, first dial the **e a r a   d o c e.**

   _____

5. I need **s s s a n e a i t c** with the puzzle.

   _____

6. The telephone **i e t r d r c o y** is that thick heavy book.

   _____

7. Jim got the flu and had to **c n c l a e** his vacation.

   _____

8. The phone **p r t r o e a o** helped me place the call.

   _____

9. Keep your doctor's number by the phone in case of

   y c g r e n e e m. _____

10. My brother is a firefighter and my sister a **i o e p l c** officer.

    _____

Vocabulary: Meaning and Message © Fearon/Janus Publishers

Lesson 4, Exercise 5
Dictionary Skills: Syllables

Name _____ Date _____

Some words are long and hard to pronounce. For instance, can you pronounce these words?

locomotive   pentathlon   imperturbable

If you can't, you're not alone. Many people have a hard time knowing how to pronounce them. One way to learn how to pronounce a word is to study how it is divided into parts, or syllables.

Dictionaries include words that have been broken into syllables. Here are the words from above as they would appear in a dictionary entry. Say each syllable softly out loud. Then put the syllables all together and say the whole word.

lo co mo tive   **pen tath lon**   **im per turb a ble**

Look up each word below in a dictionary. Write it in syllables on the line.

1. **assistance** _____

2. **cancel** _____

3. **collect** _____

4. **directory** _____

5. **discount** _____

6. **emergency** _____

7. **distance** _____

8. **operator** _____

9. **police** _____

10. **area** _____

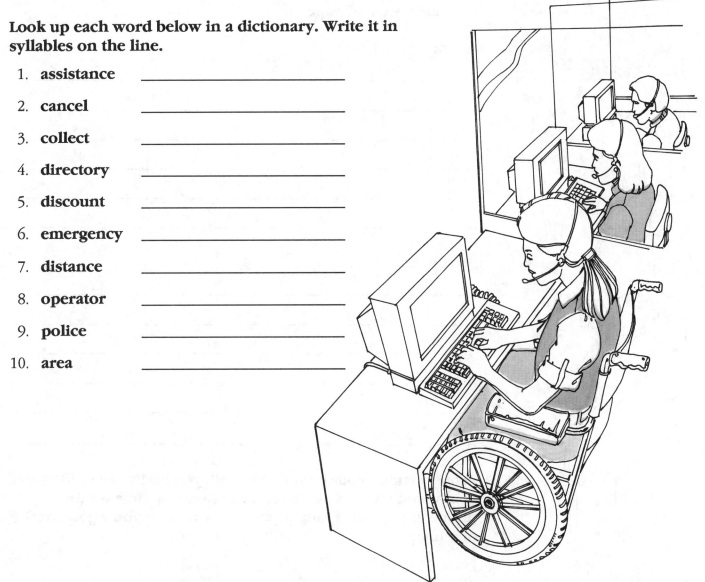

Vocabulary: Meaning and Message © Fearon/Janus Publishers

Writing on Your Own

Name _____ Date _____

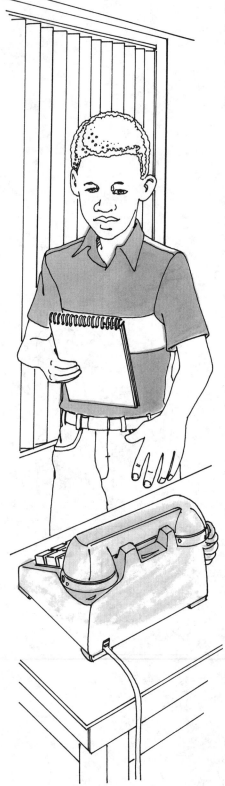

Suppose you can make two long distance phone calls anywhere in the world. Write down the names of two people you would like to call. They can be people you know or people you've never met. You might want to talk with friends, relatives, the President of the United States, a rock star in South America, or a person your age in Japan.

_____

_____

Now write down all the things you would say to each person. Don't worry about writing perfect sentences. Just try to get your thoughts down on paper. If you need more room, use separate sheets of paper.

Person #1:

_____

_____

_____

_____

_____

_____

Person #2:

_____

_____

_____

_____

_____

_____

Before making your next phone call, you might try doing what you've done in this exercise. It can save you time on the phone. If the call is long distance, it can save you a good deal of money.

Lesson 4, Exercise 7
Test

Name _____ Date _____

Choose the best word to complete each sentence.

1. Joy couldn't do it alone. She needed _____.

   A. distance   B. assistance   C. operator   D. discount

2. Many stores offer _____ in January.

   A. discounts   B. emergency   C. distance   D. collect

3. Do you know Maria's _____ in California?

   A. operator   B. distance   C. emergency   D. area code

4. If you dial 0, you'll get the _____.

   A. operator   B. distance   C. emergency   D. police

5. A fight started, but the _____ broke it up.

   A. emergency   B. operator   C. directory   D. police

6. The rain forced us to _____ our picnic.

   A. assist   B. cancel   C. discount   D. collect

7. Hand me the _____ of names and addresses.

   A. directory   B. operator   C. area code   D. police

8. Our phone bill was high because we accepted too many _____ calls.

   A. discount   B. code   C. collect   D. assist

9. The fire department responded to the _____.

   A. area code   B. emergency   C. directory   D. discount

10. It's a long _____ from here to there.

   A. distance   B. area code   C. discount   D. collect

Vocabulary: Meaning and Message © Fearon/Janus Publishers

Unit 1 Review

Name _____ Date _____

A. Darken the circled letter beside the word that is being described.

1. to go away
   - (A) warning
   - (B) leave
   - (C) discount
   - (D) owner

2. a place where food is prepared and eaten
   - (A) restroom
   - (B) shelf
   - (C) area code
   - (D) restaurant

3. belonging to a specific person; not general
   - (A) private
   - (B) public
   - (C) appropriate
   - (D) distance

4. a group of people who keep law and order
   - (A) operators
   - (B) landlords
   - (C) police
   - (D) owners

5. to cross out
   - (A) escape
   - (B) directory
   - (C) lease
   - (D) cancel

6. the way in
   - (A) exit
   - (B) first aid
   - (C) entrance
   - (D) collect

7. help
   - (A) assistance
   - (B) property
   - (C) tenant
   - (D) warning

8. a person who keeps a building in good shape
   - (A) tenant
   - (B) superintendent
   - (C) gentleman
   - (D) operator

9. without mistakes
   - (A) closed
   - (B) out of order
   - (C) correct
   - (D) city

10. something that can cause harm
    - (A) details
    - (B) danger
    - (C) discount
    - (D) lease

11. woman
    - (A) lady
    - (B) landlord
    - (C) rent
    - (D) gentleman

12. one or more rented rooms
    - (A) tenant
    - (B) building
    - (C) landlord
    - (D) apartment

13. payment made to live in or use a house or apartment
    - (A) emergency
    - (B) rent
    - (C) sign
    - (D) property

Vocabulary: Meaning and Message © Fearon/Janus Publishers

Unit 1 Review

Name _____ Date _____

B. Find the word in each group that is not related to the other words. Darken the circled letter beside that word.

1. Ⓐ apartment
   Ⓑ landlord
   Ⓒ first aid
   Ⓓ real estate

2. Ⓐ operator
   Ⓑ assistance
   Ⓒ directory
   Ⓓ fire escape

3. Ⓐ restroom
   Ⓑ leave
   Ⓒ ladies
   Ⓓ gentlemen

4. Ⓐ police
   Ⓑ shelf
   Ⓒ emergency
   Ⓓ assistance

5. Ⓐ entrance
   Ⓑ tenant
   Ⓒ rent
   Ⓓ lease

C. Match each word on the left with its description on the right. Write the letter on the line.

1. out of order _____
2. public _____
3. sign _____
4. exit _____
5. discount _____
6. distance _____
7. area code _____
8. tenant _____
9. city _____
10. shelf _____

a. for all the people

b. the space between two points

c. three numbers that are dialed when making a non-local call

d. a person who pays rent to live in a house or apartment

e. the way out

f. a place where people live and work that is bigger than a town

g. a flat surface used for holding things

h. the amount of money taken off the usual price of an item

i. broken or not working properly

j. a board on which information is given

Reading on Your Own

Name _____ Date _____

As you read this story, think about the meaning of each highlighted word.

The School Store

Jason's school had a small store where students could buy pencils, pens, paper, and other supplies. Every month, a different student helped out in the store. In March, it was Jason's turn to work there in the mornings and afternoons.

Jason's math teacher, Mr. Strong, showed Jason what to do. He told Jason that he had two jobs. Jason would sell supplies to the students. This meant that he would be learning to use a cash **register.** Jason would also be spending some time making sure the store was kept neat and clean.

Jason quickly learned how to make **change.** If someone gave him a dollar for a $.95 item, Jason had to return five **cents.** If the item cost $.75, the change would be a **quarter,** or $.25. Jason also learned where to put the money in the register. There were certain places for paper money, the one-, five-, and ten-dollar **bills.** There were other places for coins. Pennies, **nickels, dimes,** and quarters were kept there.

Jason kept the store neat and clean while he worked, but this took only a **fraction** of his time. He spent the greater part of his time getting supplies for students, taking their money, and making change. Jason also kept a list that showed every item he had sold and how much it had cost.

At the end of his first day, Jason showed Mr. Strong his list. The **amount** at the bottom of the list was $500.00. "That can't be right!" said Mr. Strong. He looked over the list. Then he smiled.

"When you added up the money, you put the **decimal** point in the wrong place," he said. "You have to move it to the left. Today you sold fifty dollars worth of supplies—not five hundred." Jason hoped he would never make that mistake again.

If you could be a salesperson in a store, what store would it be? Why?

_____

_____

_____

Vocabulary: Meaning and Message © Fearon/Janus Publishers

Using Context

Name _____ Date _____

Circle the word that fits the definition.

1. the total or sum of two or more numbers; the whole; a quantity

   decimal   fraction   amount

2. the dot that comes before a number, used with the word *point*

   decimal   bill   change

3. a coin whose value is ten cents

   nickel   dime   total

4. a coin whose value is five cents

   fraction   nickel   decimal

5. a machine used to add up and store money

   register   fraction   dime

6. a coin whose value is twenty-five cents, or 1/4 of a dollar; any of four equal parts

   quarter   dime   nickel

7. one hundred of these equals one dollar; a penny

   dime   cent   total

8. a part of the whole, such as 1/2

   amount   fraction   dime

9. money returned to a customer who has paid more than what was owed

   change   bills   five cents

10. pieces of paper money

    bills   amounts   decimals

Vocabulary: Meaning and Message © Fearon/Janus Publishers

Lesson 1, Exercise 3
Vocabulary Development: Multiple Meanings

Name _____ Date _____

Read these sentences carefully:

Watch me while I dive into the pool.

Her watch was broken, so she couldn't tell the time.

The young soldier took the first watch over the prisoner.

What do you notice about the sentences? You may have seen that each sentence uses the word *watch* in a different way. In the first sentence, *watch* means "to look at." In the second sentence, *watch* is another word for "a timepiece." In the third sentence, *watch* means "a period of lookout duty."

Words often have a number of different meanings. The word *trunk*, for example, can mean "a box in which to store clothes." It can mean "the carrying space in the rear of a car." It can also mean "an elephant's snout."

Because a word can have more than one meaning, it is easy to become confused by the word. We might see the word *trunk*, for example, and think right away of the back of a car. However, this might not be what the person who wrote the word meant.

A. The highlighted word in each sentence below has more than one meaning. Write the meaning of the word as it is being used in the sentence. Use a dictionary if you need help.

1. Joan carefully placed the money in the **register.**

   _____

2. Will your parents **register** to vote in their new neighborhood?

   _____

3. Here's the **change** from your ten-dollar bill.

   _____

4. The leaves are beginning to **change** colors.

   _____

5. The soldiers' **quarters** are on the other side of camp.

   _____

6. Can you lend me two **quarters**?

   _____

Vocabulary: Meaning and Message © Fearon/Janus Publishers

Vocabulary Development: Multiple Meanings

Name _____ Date _____

B. Each word below has more than one meaning. Write two sentences for each word. In each sentence, use the word to show a different meaning. Use a dictionary if you need help.

1. **mean**

_____

_____

_____

_____

2. **watch**

_____

_____

_____

_____

3. **bill**

_____

_____

_____

_____

4. **exhaust**

_____

_____

_____

_____

5. **lean**

_____

_____

_____

_____

Vocabulary: Meaning and Message © Fearon/Janus Publishers

Puzzle

Name _____ Date _____

A. Read each clue. Write the letter on the line.

CLUES

1. The first letter of this word is in *bat* but not in *cat*. _____

2. The second letter of this word is in *fill* but not in *fall*. _____

3. The third letter of this word is in *light* but not in *sight*. _____

4. The fourth letter of this word is in *lip* but not in *sip*. _____

5. The fifth letter of this word is in *so* but not in *to*. _____

6. Solve the puzzle. Write the letters from above to name something that birds have.

—— —— —— —— ——

B. Follow the same directions as above.

CLUES

1. The first letter of this word is in *run* but not in *sun*. _____

2. The second letter of this word is in *are* but not in *art*. _____

3. The third letter of this word is in *go* but not in *to*. _____

4. The fourth letter of this word is in *is* but not in *as*. _____

5. The fifth letter of this word is in *set* but not in *wet*. _____

6. The sixth letter of this word is in *tea* but not in *sea*. _____

7. The seventh letter of this word is in *get* but not in *got*. _____

8. The eighth letter of this word is in *ear* but not in *eat*. _____

9. What must you do before you can vote?

—— —— —— —— —— —— —— ——

Vocabulary: Meaning and Message © Fearon/Janus Publishers

Dictionary Skills: Accented Syllables

Name _____ Date _____

Read this sentence aloud softly.

Do not *desert* me in the *desert*.

The word *desert* in this sentence has two different meanings. It also has two different pronunciations. The first *desert* is a verb that means "to leave." It is pronounced with the accent on the second syllable, *sert*. The second *desert* is a noun that means "a hot, dry place where there is little plant life." It is pronounced with the accent on the first syllable, *des*.

In a dictionary, each word is broken into syllables. An accent mark shows which syllable should be pronounced with the most stress, or loudness. Here are some examples:

ex plain′   grate′ful   im press′   mon′ ster

Some words in the dictionary have two accent marks, one heavy (′) and one light (′). The heavy accent mark shows which syllable gets the most stress. The light accent mark shows which syllable gets the second-most stress. Let's look at the word *auditorium*. Here is how the word is broken into syllables:

au′ di to′ ri um

The heavy accent mark beside *to* shows that you pronounce that syllable with the most stress. The light accent mark beside *au* shows that you pronounce that syllable with the next-most stress. The three syllables without accent marks are pronounced the least strongly. They are pronounced with equal strength.

Here are 10 words divided into syllables. Five have the accent marks on the correct syllables. Five do not. Say each word quietly. Rewrite the words that have accents on the incorrect syllables. Place each accent mark in the correct place.

1. a′ mount _____
2. frac′ tion _____
3. nick el′ _____
4. quar′ ter _____
5. dec′ i mal _____
6. pen′ cil _____
7. i′ tem _____
8. num ber′ _____
9. re′ turn _____
10. in′ clude _____

Writing on Your Own

Name _____ Date _____

Suppose you work after school in a store. It sells clothing, shoes, cosmetics, jewelry, appliances, records, tapes, and CDs. What part of the store would you most like to work in?

_____

Imagine that a customer brings you an item and wants to know more about it. First, think of something that could be sold in your part of the store. For example, in the clothing department, it might be a winter coat. In the shoe department, it could be a pair of boots. In the appliance department, it could be a microwave oven. Write the name of the item here.

_____

Now make up as many details about the item as you can. They can include what it's made of, how it is cared for, the price, and so on.

_____

_____

_____

_____

_____

The customer listens carefully but is still not sure whether or not to buy it. Try to get the customer to see that the item is the one for him or her. Write one or two statements to convince the customer to buy it.

_____

_____

_____

_____

_____

Test

Name _____ Date _____

Choose the best word to complete each sentence.

1. The librarian spends only a _____ of her time reading to children.

   A. fraction   B. change   C. decimal   D. dime

2. All the new buildings in our city have really _____ the skyline.

   A. changed   B. amounted   C. registered   D. fractioned

3. I have three one-dollar _____ in my wallet.

   A. nickels   B. quarters   C. dimes   D. bills

4. What _____ of money did I lend you?

   A. register   B. amount   C. cents   D. quarter

5. I have no more money—not a _____!

   A. bills   B. fractions   C. register   D. cent

6. Can you give me four _____ for a dollar?

   A. dimes   B. nickels   C. bills   D. quarters

7. When we studied fractions and _____, I found out that half a dollar can be written as $.50.

   A. amount   B. nickels   C. decimals   D. change

8. This roll of fifty _____ is worth five dollars.

   A. amounts   B. fractions   C. dimes   D. bills

9. Pay this bill at the cash _____.

   A. register   B. fraction   C. decimal   D. quarter

10. Twenty _____ are worth the same as a dollar.

    A. bills   B. nickels   C. registers   D. decimals

As you read this story, think about the meaning of each highlighted word.

At the Bank

It was career day at Irene's school. Every year, students chose a different workplace to visit. This year, Irene was going to a bank. At the bank, Irene met Ms. Barker, one of the bank's officers.

Ms. Barker told Irene how the bank worked. "People deposit, or store, money here. The bank keeps records of how much they deposit. If they want to take some of their money out of the bank, they **withdraw** it. If they want to **borrow** money, they can do that, too. It's called taking out a **loan.** The bank will supply the money for, or **finance,** different kinds of loans. If you want to buy a house, you can take out a **mortgage.** In simple terms, this means that the bank buys the house. When you pay off the mortgage by repaying the bank, the house belongs to you."

"Do people have to pay to borrow money?" Irene **inquired.**

"Yes, they do," replied Ms. Barker. "We charge **interest.** That's one of the ways the bank makes money. We also *pay* interest to people who have savings accounts here. They earn a small amount of money for keeping their money in the bank.

"In order to **manage,** or control, their money, most people use checking accounts," Ms. Barker continued. "If you write a check to someone, the bank will pay that person the amount of money you wrote. At the end of each month, the bank sends you a record of all the checks you've written. This record is called a *statement*. It shows how much money is left in your checking account. This amount is called the **balance.**

"If you have a checking account and someone gives you a check, you can either cash it or deposit it in your account. First, however, you must **endorse** it, or sign your name on the back of it."

When Irene left the bank, she thanked Ms. Barker for all her help. On her way home, Irene thought that she'd probably like to work in a bank herself someday.

What question about banks would you most like to ask?

_____

_____

_____

Vocabulary: Meaning and Message © Fearon/Janus Publishers

Using Context

Name _____ Date _____

Circle the word that best completes each sentence.

1. My brother asked my parents if he could _____ their car.

   mortgage   withdraw   borrow   endorse

2. Anita's bank _____ the loan for her new car.

   financed   inquiry   interest   withdrew

3. In the last year, Jane's $100.00 earned $6.00 in _____.

   loan   withdrawal   endorsement   interest

4. Only a very good babysitter can _____ these children.

   withdraw   mortgage   manage   inquire

5. To buy a new bike, Ted _____ $200.00 from his savings account.

   withdrew   mortgaged   inquired   managed

6. The weight on one side of the seesaw was _____ by the weight on the other.

   mortgaged   balanced   borrowed   endorsed

7. When I deposited the check, I _____ it on the back.

   loaned   inquired   endorsed   withdrew

8. If you don't know where to go, _____ at the information desk.

   inquire   balance   borrow   loan

9. I'll have to take out a _____ to pay these bills.

   withdraw   balance   interest   loan

10. It took 30 years to pay off the _____, but now the house is ours.

    endorsement   inquiry   withdrawal   mortgage

Vocabulary: Meaning and Message © Fearon/Janus Publishers

Vocabulary Development: Suffixes

Name _____ Date _____

Notice what happens when you add the letters *ly* to the word *sad*. The result is a new word, *sadly*. The words *sad* and *sadly* are related. They both refer to the feeling of unhappiness, but they are also different. *Sad* describes a person, place, or thing.

We were *sad* when our team lost the game.

Sadly describes how something is done.

The team walked *sadly* off the field after losing the game.

The letters *ly* form a **suffix.** Suffixes are groups of letters that are added to the ends of words. When added to words, suffixes give the words different meanings. Here are some common suffixes. Notice how they change the meanings of the words when they are added.

Word	Suffix	Meaning of Suffix	New Word
happy	-ly	in a certain manner	happily
treat	-ment	result; action	treatment
fiction	-al	relating to	fictional
hunt	-er	one who does	hunter
train	-ee	one who receives an action	trainee
health	-y	having; characterized by	healthy

Look at the word *fiction* in the list above. It is a noun that means "a story that has been made up or invented." The word *fictional* is an adjective that describes a story that is made up or invented. A work of fiction, such as a novel, is a fictional work.

The verb *train* means "to instruct or teach." The word *trainee* is a noun. A trainee is a person who receives instruction. The word *trainer* is also a noun. It means "one who trains." We could say that a trainer trains a trainee.

Adding a suffix to a word can change the word's spelling. Notice the word *happy* above. You change the *y* to *i* before adding *ly*. If you're not sure how to spell a word when you're adding a suffix to it, check a dictionary.

Vocabulary: Meaning and Message © Fearon/Janus Publishers

Vocabulary Development: Suffixes

Name _____ Date _____

Combine these words and suffixes to make new words. Then use each new word in a sentence. Follow the instructions for changing the spelling of some words.

1. **endorse + ment =** _____

_____

_____

2. **borrow + er =** _____

_____

_____

3. **mortgage + ee =** _____ (Drop the *e* in *mortgage* before adding *ee*.)

_____

_____

4. **withdraw + al =** _____

_____

_____

5. **inquire + y =** _____ (Drop the *e* in *inquire* before adding *y*.)

_____

_____

6. **manage + ment=** _____

_____

_____

7. **trick + y=** _____

_____

_____

Puzzle

Name _____ Date _____

Use the clues to help you complete the crossword puzzle. The answers can be found in the box.

borrow	mortgage	withdraw	finance	loan
interest	manage	balance	endorse	inquire

Across
1. how much is left
5. to lend
6. to provide money for
8. something a bank holds
9. to take out

Down
1. to use something for a while
2. to control or direct
3. to sign the back of a check
4. what your money can earn
7. to ask

Lesson 2, Exercise 5
Dictionary Skills: Pronunciation

Name _____ Date _____

You can probably pronounce most of the words you read. Some, however, may give you difficulty. For instance, can you pronounce these words correctly?

ermine   essential   equatorial

You can find out how to pronounce these words by studying their pronunciation spellings in a dictionary:

ûr´ min   i sen´ shəl   ē´ kwə tor´ ē əl

The symbols used in pronunciation spellings show the many different sounds we speak. To find out what the symbols mean, look at the pronunciation key below. A pronunciation key usually appears at the bottom of every right-hand dictionary page or at the front of the dictionary.

at; **ā**te; **tä**r; **shâ**re; **e**nd; **wē**; **i**n; **ī**ce; **fî**erce; **no**t; **sō**; **lô**ng; **oi**l; **ou**r; **u**p; **ū**se; **trü**e; **pu̇**t; **bû**rn; **ch**ew; **wi**ng; **sh**oe; **bo**th; **th**is; **hw** in **wh**ich; **zh** in treasure; **ə** in **a**bout, **a**gent, penc**i**l, **c**ollect, foc**u**s

Look at the pronunciation spelling of the word *ermine*. Then study the pronunciation key. Find a *u* with the symbol ^ over it. Now you can see that the *e* in *ermine* is pronounced like the *u* in *burn*.

Look at the pronunciation spelling of *essential* and, again, study the pronunciation key. You will see that the *e* in *essential* is pronounced like the *i* in *in*.

The pronunciation spelling of *equatorial* shows yet a third way to pronounce the letter *e*. Here it sounds like the *e* in *we*.

The pronunciation spellings for the words *essential* and *equatorial* include a symbol that looks like an upside-down *e*. This symbol is called a *schwa* (pronounced *shwah*). The schwa is pronounced *uh*, as in the word *about*.

Write the word for each of these pronunciation spellings.

1. bal´ əns   _____

2. man´ ij   _____

3. en dôrs´   _____

4. in kwīr´   _____

5. with drô´   _____

Writing on Your Own

Name _____ Date _____

Imagine that your class will soon be holding a career day. Each student gets to vote on the workplace that the class will visit. List a few places where you might one day like to work.

_____

_____

_____

Look over your list. Pick the one place that most interests you. Put a check mark beside it. Now make notes of ideas that will convince your classmates to visit the place you have chosen. List your reasons here.

_____

_____

_____

_____

Suppose that your workplace has been chosen as the best one to visit on career day. It's now up to you to write to the person in charge there. Ask if you can visit. Tell why it is important to your class. Remember to be polite. Write a first draft of your letter on a separate sheet of paper. Then write a final version below or on another sheet of paper.

_____

_____

_____

_____

_____

_____

_____

Vocabulary: Meaning and Message © Fearon/Janus Publishers

Test

Name _____ Date _____

Choose the best word to fit each definition.

1. the part that is left over; also, to make things equal; to hold steady

   A. inquire   B. withdraw   C. balance   D. loan

2. to ask questions about something

   A. inquire   B. loan   C. endorse   D. mortgage

3. to sign one's name on the back of a check

   A. withdraw   B. loan   C. inquire   D. endorse

4. to lend something; also, that which is lent

   A. manage   B. loan   C. mortgage   D. borrow

5. to take away or remove, as money from a bank; also, to go away

   A. withdraw   B. manage   C. finance   D. endorse

6. to take something that will later be returned

   A. endorse   B. borrow   C. finance   D. loan

7. to provide money for something, as a bank might do

   A. mortgage   B. endorse   C. finance   D. inquire

8. money paid for the use of money

   A. interest   B. loan   C. mortgage   D. finance

9. to direct or control

   A. inquire   B. withdraw   C. borrow   D. manage

10. a means of borrowing money; the ownership of property by a bank until the person buying the property has repaid the bank's loan

    A. inquiry   B. manage   C. finance   D. mortgage

Vocabulary: Meaning and Message © Fearon/Janus Publishers

Reading on Your Own

Name _____ Date _____

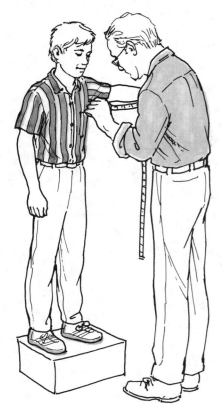

As you read this story, think about the meaning of each highlighted word.

Inch by Inch

How far do you live from Chicago? How tall are you? How much cloth would you need to **add** a border to a new dress? These questions can be answered with different units of **measurement.** For example, the distance between two cities is measured in miles. A person's height is measured in feet and inches.

A very long time ago, it was **difficult** to talk about lengths and distances. People didn't have the words to measure them. As time passed, people tried to use units of measurement everyone could understand. In ancient Rome, for example, the unit of measurement for distance was a person's foot. This was not very exact, since the sizes of people's feet **varied** greatly. Today we use the term "foot" to mean exactly 12 inches. The Romans also used other parts of the body as measuring units. The length of the index finger from the tip to the first joint was an inch. A yard was **equal** to the length of an **average** person's arm. A "pace" was two steps, and a mile was 1,000 paces.

Today, we have exact standards of measurement. Anyone who makes a ruler, yardstick, or tape measure must follow them. Without the standards, we might not **agree** on exactly how long an inch, a foot, or a yard should be.

Many countries use the **metric** system of measurement. The metric system is based on the number ten. There are ten millimeters to a centimeter, ten centimeters to a decimeter, and ten decimeters to a meter. A meter is equal to 39.37 inches.

Some people say the metric system is **less** difficult than our own. Attempts to change our system, however, have not been **successful.**

What is the longest distance you have ever traveled? Where did you go?

_____

_____

_____

Vocabulary: Meaning and Message © Fearon/Janus Publishers

Using Context

Name _____ Date _____

Circle the word that fits the definition.

1. to say yes to; to have the same opinion as another

   add   difficult   agree

2. not easy; hard

   vary   successful   difficult

3. having a favorable result

   successful   less   difficult

4. to make different; to be different

   measurement   vary   equal

5. to increase or make larger; to combine

   less   add   vary

6. usual or normal

   average   equal   less

7. smaller in amount or size

   less   vary   measurement

8. the same in amount or size

   average   equal   successful

9. the act of finding out the amount, size, or weight of something

   measurement   equal   average

10. having to do with a measurement system based on tens

    average   metric   add

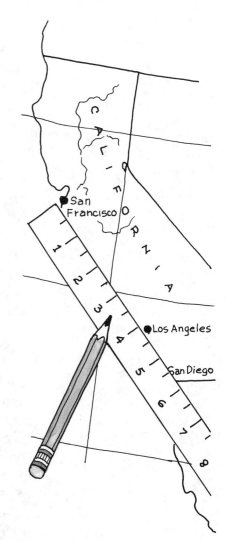

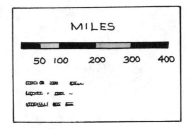

MILES

50 100   200   300   400

Vocabulary Development: Antonyms

Name _____ Date _____

What do you notice about these pairs of words?

empty—full   kind—cruel   ugly—beautiful

You probably noticed that the words in each pair are opposites. Words whose meanings are opposite to each other are called **antonyms.**

Here are some other antonyms:

long—short   war—peace   wonderful—terrible

Not all words have antonyms. For example, what would be the opposite of the word *movie*? There isn't one. There are more antonyms for adjectives and adverbs than there are for nouns, pronouns, and verbs.

Antonyms can be found in many dictionaries. The abbreviation **ant.** stands for "antonym." A list of antonyms will usually be found after a list of synonyms, which are words that mean the same or nearly the same. The abbreviation for "synonym" is **syn.** If you look up the word *difficult* in a dictionary, you might find these antonyms:

easy, simple, effortless

It can be difficult to know which words are actually opposite each other in meaning. For example, you might think that an antonym for *warm* is *freezing*. However, *warm* means "moderately hot." *Freezing* means "extremely cold." So *warm* and *freezing* are not antonyms. Antonyms for *warm* include "cool" and "chilly." Try to be exact when using antonyms.

A. Find an antonym for each highlighted word below. Use a dictionary if you need help. Then rewrite the sentence using the antonym.

1. The band **agreed** on how much money to charge for their show.

_____

_____

2. Our efforts at raising money for the school were **successful.**

_____

_____

Vocabulary: Meaning and Message © Fearon/Janus Publishers

Vocabulary Development: Antonyms

Name _____ Date _____

3. The pizza was cut into six **equal** pieces.

_____

_____

4. Today I have **less** time to study than I had yesterday.

_____

_____

B. Find an antonym for each word below. Use a dictionary if you need help. Then write a sentence using the antonym.

1. **ending** _____

_____

2. **difficult** _____

_____

3. **success** _____

_____

4. **friend** _____

_____

5. **kind** _____

_____

6. **short** _____

_____

7. **huge** _____

_____

8. **new** _____

_____

Puzzle

Name _____ Date _____

Use the clues to help you complete the crossword puzzle. The answers can be found in the box.

measure	add	agree	difficult	vary
successful	average	equal	metric	less

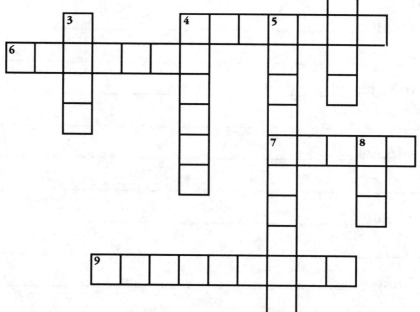

Across
1. to change
4. to figure the size of
6. most common
7. the same as
9. hard to do

Down
2. to have the same opinion
3. fewer
4. a way of measuring
5. rewarding
8. to put one thing on another

Vocabulary: Meaning and Message © Fearon/Janus Publishers

Dictionary Skills: Word Origins

Name _____ Date _____

More than half the words in our modern English vocabulary come from Latin words. Latin was the language spoken in ancient Rome. For example, the word *hibernate* means "to spend the winter sleeping." It comes from a Latin word meaning "winter quarters." *Calendar* comes from a Latin word meaning "the first day of the month." Other words in the English language are taken from many different languages and groups of people.

The names of many states come from native American languages. *Mississippi* means "big river" and "great water." *Missouri* means "people with the big canoes." *Minnesota* means "water the color of the sky." *Massachusetts* means "at the big hill." *Kentucky* means "flat land."

Some words come from the names of real or imaginary beings. The Romans named the month of January after Janus, their god of gates and doors. Janus was a two-faced god who looked in opposite directions. The holiday honoring him was probably celebrated in the month of January. It is then that we look both forward to the year that will come and backward to the year that has passed.

The word *frankfurter* is taken from a German word meaning "from Frankfurt." Frankfurt is a city in Germany. The first hot dog may have been eaten there.

Knowing the origins of words can help us figure out the meanings of unfamiliar words. For example, let's say you know that the word *astronaut* comes from two Greek words meaning "star" and "sailor." You might then figure out that *astronomy* also has something to do with the stars.

Choose the word that is being described.

> **apartment   agree   property**

1. It comes from the Latin word *proprius*. The word means "one's own." _____

2. It comes from the Italian word *appartare*. The word means "to separate." _____

3. It comes from the French word *agréer*. This word means "to receive kindly." _____

Writing on Your Own

Name _____ Date _____

Modern forms of transportation have made traveling easier than it once was. In ages past, people traveled less often than they do today. Usually, they also traveled shorter distances. Today it is not unusual for people to travel to the other side of the world. Some have even traveled into space.

Suppose that you can take two trips to anywhere you want to go. First, think of a place you would like to go to that is near your home. Where would you go that is nearby?

_____

How would you get there? Why would you choose this means of transportation?

_____

_____

Why would you want to go to this place?

_____

_____

_____

Now think of a place that is far away. Remember, you can go anywhere you want. What place would you choose?

_____

What form of transportation would you use to get there? Why?

_____

_____

What is it about this place that interests you? What would you do there? If you need more room, use another sheet of paper.

_____

_____

_____

Vocabulary: Meaning and Message © Fearon/Janus Publishers

Test

Name _____ Date _____

Choose the best word to complete each sentence.

1. The temperature here _____ from day to day.

   A. successes   B. varies   C. measures   D. adds

2. It will taste too sweet if you _____ more honey.

   A. average   B. measure   C. vary   D. add

3. We all weigh nearly the same. The _____ is 97 pounds.

   A. difficult   B. average   C. equal   D. less

4. Is there nothing we can _____ on?

   A. vary   B. average   C. difficult   D. agree

5. Mike earned a good salary and felt _____.

   A. measure   B. less   C. add   D. successful

6. Loud noises make studying _____.

   A. added   B. difficult   C. metric   D. average

7. The length of a square is _____ to its width.

   A. vary   B. less   C. metric   D. equal

8. John used a yardstick to find the room's _____.

   A. metric   B. equal   C. agree   D. measurements

9. Jesse now works fewer hours and earns _____ money.

   A. less   B. difficult   C. varied   D. metric

10. Meters and centimeters are units of measurement in the _____ system.

    A. metric   B. success   C. agree   D. less

Reading on Your Own

Name _____ Date _____

As you read this story, think about the meaning of each highlighted word.

What Day Is It?

Calendars help us measure time. Imagine what life would be like without them. How would we know how many days, **weeks,** and **months** there were before summer vacation?

One of the earliest calendars was created by ancient Egyptians. The Egyptians knew that the best time to plant crops was during the overflowing of the Nile River. This happened once a year. They observed that the moon rose 12 times **between** one overflowing and the next. Therefore, each rising moon would mark a new month.

Later, the Egyptians **identified** a certain star that appeared every year at the time of the Nile's overflowing. They **calculated** the days between the appearances of the star. The number of days they counted was 365. So the Egyptians decided that a year was made up of 365 days. Dividing 365 by 12, they created months that lasted 30 days, with five extra days at the end of the year.

The Roman calendar was developed centuries later. The Egyptian and Roman calendars were **alike** in many ways, but the Roman calendar was based on the number of days—365¼—the earth takes to move around the sun. That extra fourth of a day caused some confusion, so in 46 B.C., the Roman emperor Julius Caesar solved the problem. He ordered that every year would have only 365 days. Every fourth year, however, would **contain** 366 days. Today this is known as the leap year. In a leap year, we add a **single** day to the month of February. February has **fewer** days than the other months. In three out of every four years, it is only 28 days.

Still there were problems! The Roman system allowed "extra" days to pile up every so often. In 1582, Pope Gregory XIII declared that there would be no leap year at the end of every century. The exceptions would be those centuries that could be divided by 400. That is why 1700, 1800, and 1900 were not leap years, but 2000 will be a leap year. Pope Gregory's system is known as the Gregorian calendar. It is the one we use today.

What three important dates would you circle on your calendar? Why?

_____

_____

_____

Lesson 4, Exercise 2
Using Context

Name _____ Date _____

Circle the word that best completes each sentence.

1. Mark your birthday on the _____.

   week   month   single   calendar

2. The twins look exactly _____.

   single   identify   alike   between

3. There are 31 days in this _____.

   month   calendar   week   identify

4. Let's divide the cost _____ the two of us.

   alike   between   fewer   single

5. Flo's fish tank _____ seven goldfish.

   singles   between   calendars   contains

6. We caught more fish when _____ people were fishing.

   identify   fewer   between   single

7. There are 52 _____ in a year.

   months   calendars   weeks   fewer

8. He is unmarried and wants to remain _____.

   single   between   calculated   few

9. The gardener can _____ these plants for us.

   calculate   contain   identify   alike

10. I'll need a map to _____ the distance.

    between   calculate   contain   single

Vocabulary: Meaning and Message © Fearon/Janus Publishers

Vocabulary Development: Synonyms

Name _____ Date _____

On page 56, you learned about antonyms, which are words whose meanings are opposite each other. A **synonym** is a word that has the same or nearly the same meaning as another word. Can you think of a synonym for *run?* Here are a few examples: dash, dart, race, jog, trot.

Knowing synonyms can help you avoid using the same word over and over in your conversations and writing. Here is how a person who doesn't know any synonyms for *run* might write a paragraph:

Jody ran down the street. Then she ran into the park and through the grove of trees. She ran faster when she got near the fountain. Then she ran down Main Street and ran up the hill until she was too tired to run anymore.

Because the same word is used over and over, the sentences above are rather dull. Here is how the paragraph might be rewritten using some synonyms:

Jody raced down the street. Then she dashed into the park and through the grove of trees. She sped up when she got near the fountain. Then she hurried down Main Street and darted up the hill until she was too tired to run anymore.

As you can see, the second paragraph is livelier. You wouldn't want to wear the same shirt every day or watch the same TV show over and over. So, too, you wouldn't want to repeat the same word too often. Repetition can get boring.

Synonyms can be found in many dictionaries. Look for the abbreviation **syn.** after the definition of the word. Another place to find synonyms is in a thesaurus. A thesaurus lists many synonyms for each entry word. However, it does not define the word.

A. Circle the letter beside the synonym for each highlighted word below. Then use the synonym in a sentence.

1. **alike**   a. similar   b. unusual   c. pleasant

_____

_____

2. **contain**   a. empty   b. jar   c. hold

_____

_____

Vocabulary Development: Synonyms

Name _____ Date _____

3. **identify** a. accuse b. recognize c. welcome

_____

_____

4. **system** a. method b. year c. number

_____

_____

B. Find synonyms for the highlighted words below. Then rewrite the sentences with the synonyms you chose.

1. Can you **calculate** the number of weeks left until vacation?

_____

_____

2. After everyone had eaten breakfast, only **a single** muffin remained in the box.

_____

_____

3. This basketball star **jumped** high to score the winning points.

_____

_____

4. We saw a terrific movie last week, but the one we watched tonight was **bad.**

_____

_____

5. Because we came so close to losing, the game has been **interesting.**

_____

_____

6. He has been **eating** those chips throughout the entire show.

_____

_____

Puzzle

Name _____ Date _____

The words in the box can be found in the puzzle below. They
may be written in any direction. Find and circle each one. You
may want to check off each word in the box after you have
circled it. One word has been circled and checked as an
example.

contain	month	identify	✔calculate	single
alike	calendar	between	fewer	week

```
c a l c u l a t e e r i
a w a r c t u c p d e d
l h e j h m g n h p p e
e v y e n o x t z r w n
n v r t k p n t e e v t
d a d t y o a l i k e i
a u i k m s i n g l e f
r b e t w e e n n i o y
f e w e r f g r m p c y
f r p t c o n t a i n v
```

Vocabulary: Meaning and Message © Fearon/Janus Publishers

Word Power: Nouns

Name _____ Date _____

Here's a short quiz. Complete it quickly.

> Name five people.
> Name five places.
> Name five things.

Congratulations! You have just come up with fifteen nouns.

Nouns are one of our language's eight parts of speech. The other seven are *nouns, pronouns, verbs, adjectives, adverbs, conjunctions, prepositions,* and *interjections*. Every word fits into one of these groups. Dictionaries tell which part of speech a word is. Most dictionaries abbreviate the parts of speech like this:

noun—**n.**	verb—**v.**	preposition—**prep.**
pronoun—**pro.**	adverb—**adv.**	interjection—**interj.**
adjective—**adj.**	conjunction—**conj.**	

Nouns are naming words for persons, places, things, events, and ideas. Here are some examples:

emperor—Julius	country—Egypt	month—July
holiday—New Year's Day	language— English	

You probably noticed that some of the nouns above begin with small letters. Others begin with capital letters. Those that begin with small letters are called *common nouns*. Common nouns name persons, places, things, events, or ideas. The nouns above that begin with capital letters are called *proper nouns*. They name *particular,* or *specific,* persons, places, things, events, and ideas. Here are some more examples of both common and proper nouns:

Common nouns:	actor	river	book
Proper nouns:	Bill Cosby	Nile	*My Life*

Follow the instructions for writing sentences. Then underline all the nouns in each sentence. Underline the common nouns once. Underline the proper nouns twice.

1. Write a sentence about your school.

_____

2. Write a sentence about something you ate today.

_____

3. Write a sentence about someone in your family.

_____

Vocabulary: Meaning and Message © Fearon/Janus Publishers

Writing on Your Own

Name _____ Date _____

Some of our memories are stronger than others. There have probably been several events in your life that still stand out in your mind. What do you recall as having had a real impact on your life? Seeing an old friend again or passing a difficult test may have left you feeling happy. Getting sick or saying good-bye to someone may have left you feeling sad. Some events leave us feeling happy one moment and sad the next.

Think of three events or moments that stand out in your mind. Write down the date on which each event took place. If you don't recall the exact date, come as close as you can. If necessary, write something like, "About two years ago, . . ." Then explain the event. Tell why this was, or still is, an important date for you.

If you need more room, use one or more separate sheets of paper.

1. _____

_____

_____

_____

2. _____

_____

_____

_____

3. _____

_____

_____

_____

Vocabulary: Meaning and Message © Fearon/Janus Publishers

Lesson 4, Exercise 7
Test

Name _____ Date _____

Choose the best word to fit each definition.

1. seven days

   A. calendar   B. fewer   C. month   D. week

2. one of the twelve parts of the year

   A. alike   B. week   C. month   D. calendar

3. a chart of the days, weeks, and months in the year; a list of events that will take place

   A. calendar   B. calculate   C. between   D. contain

4. in the space or time that separates two things

   A. alike   B. between   C. fewer   D. month

5. in a similar way; like something or someone else

   A. single   B. fewer   C. week   D. alike

6. to figure out, usually by using mathematics

   A. calendar   B. calculate   C. identify   D. contain

7. not as many as

   A. contain   B. identify   C. fewer   D. alike

8. to hold or enclose; to be made up of

   A. contain   B. calculate   C. identify   D. between

9. only one; not married

   A. alike   B. fewer   C. single   D. between

10. to recognize; to point out; to name

    A. calculate   B. identify   C. month   D. alike

Unit 2 Review

Name _____ Date _____

**A. Find the word in each group that is not related to the other words.
Darken the circled letter beside that word.**

1. Ⓐ withdraw
   Ⓑ balance
   Ⓒ borrow
   Ⓓ calender

2. Ⓐ vary
   Ⓑ dime
   Ⓒ nickel
   Ⓓ quarter

3. Ⓐ bills
   Ⓑ alike
   Ⓒ change
   Ⓓ cents

4. Ⓐ calendar
   Ⓑ month
   Ⓒ add
   Ⓓ week

5. Ⓐ interest
   Ⓑ identify
   Ⓒ loan
   Ⓓ finance

6. Ⓐ add
   Ⓑ average
   Ⓒ measurement
   Ⓓ success

B. Darken the circled letter beside the word that is being described.

1. to sign one's name on the back of a check
   Ⓐ inquire
   Ⓑ endorse
   Ⓒ mortgage
   Ⓓ manage

2. to share an idea about something
   Ⓐ difficult
   Ⓑ vary
   Ⓒ agree
   Ⓓ contain

3. the sum of two or more quantities
   Ⓐ amount
   Ⓑ decimal
   Ⓒ metric
   Ⓓ fraction

4. one
   Ⓐ metric
   Ⓑ calculate
   Ⓒ fewer
   Ⓓ single

5. to put one onto another
   Ⓐ between
   Ⓑ successful
   Ⓒ add
   Ⓓ equal

6. a machine that adds
   Ⓐ metric
   Ⓑ amount
   Ⓒ register
   Ⓓ mortgage

7. to take out
   Ⓐ mortgage
   Ⓑ endorse
   Ⓒ balance
   Ⓓ withdraw

8. to provide money
   Ⓐ agree
   Ⓑ finance
   Ⓒ contain
   Ⓓ identify

Vocabulary: Meaning and Message © Fearon/Janus Publishers

Unit 2 Review

9. seven days
   - (A) week
   - (B) month
   - (C) calendar
   - (D) single

10. similar
    - (A) fewer
    - (B) identify
    - (C) alike
    - (D) inquire

C. Choose the word or phrase that means about the same as the highlighted word. Darken the circled letter.

1. six **cents**
   - (A) pennies
   - (B) dimes
   - (C) nickels
   - (D) quarters

2. **difficult** decision
   - (A) measured
   - (B) hard
   - (C) financial
   - (D) appropriate

3. **fewer** students
   - (A) not as many
   - (B) average
   - (C) private
   - (D) public

4. above **average**
   - (A) monthly
   - (B) decimal
   - (C) normal
   - (D) canceled

5. **equal** amounts
   - (A) different
   - (B) decimal
   - (C) varied
   - (D) same

6. **identify** the criminal
   - (A) measure
   - (B) endorse
   - (C) point out
   - (D) collect

7. **fraction** of the whole
   - (A) container
   - (B) part
   - (C) discount
   - (D) mortgage

8. **loan** a coat
   - (A) lend
   - (B) inquire
   - (C) balance
   - (D) leave

9. **manage** poorly
   - (A) interest
   - (B) private
   - (C) direct
   - (D) dangerous

10. **calculate** the total
    - (A) figure out
    - (B) average
    - (C) equal
    - (D) borrow

11. small **balance**
    - (A) endorsement
    - (B) amount left
    - (C) exact change
    - (D) register

12. **contains** iron
    - (A) includes
    - (B) measurement
    - (C) mortgage
    - (D) finance

13. the road **between** Boston and New York
    - (A) joining
    - (B) alike
    - (C) add
    - (D) average

Vocabulary: Meaning and Message © Fearon/Janus Publishers

As you read this story, think about the meaning of each highlighted word.

Writing the Constitution

In 1787, the United States was a very young country. Only eleven years before, it had won its **independence,** or freedom, from England. Now, the new country's political leaders decided it was time for a strong central government.

Fifty-five men gathered in Philadelphia in 1787. They were sent by 12 of the original 13 states. Rhode Island was the only one that didn't send a **delegate.** The plan was to write the **Constitution** of the United States. This would become our country's basic set of laws.

The Constitution created three separate parts, or branches, of government: the **executive,** the legislative, and the judicial. The executive branch is headed by the president. It sees that the laws are carried out. The legislative branch writes new laws. The judicial branch interprets, or gives meaning to, the laws.

The legislative branch is made up of the two "houses" of **Congress,** the **Senate** and the **House of Representatives.** In the Senate, each state has two members, called senators. The number of representatives a state has in the House of Representatives depends on the number of people who live in that state. Larger states have more representatives than smaller states.

The judicial branch, or the **judiciary,** is the system of federal courts. The highest court in the land is the Supreme Court. It has the final say on arguments about the law.

In 1791, the **Bill of Rights** was added to the Constitution. The Bill of Rights is made up of ten additions, or **amendments,** to the Constitution. They define and protect our basic rights, or freedoms. Among them are freedom of speech, freedom of the press, freedom of religion, and the right to a fair trial.

The Constitution has changed over the years as many amendments have been added to it. It remains, however, as the foundation upon which our entire system of government is built.

Which of the rights mentioned above do you think is the most important? Why?

_____

_____

_____

Vocabulary: Meaning and Message © Fearon/Janus Publishers

Lesson 1, Exercise 2
Using Context

Name _____ Date _____

Circle the word that is being described.

1. a person chosen to speak or act for others

   judiciary   independence   delegate

2. the legislative branch of the government. It writes new laws.

   Bill of Rights   executive   Congress

3. the part of Congress that has two lawmakers from each state

   Senate   House of Representatives   amendment

4. the part of Congress whose membership is based on the number of people living in a state

   Senate   House of Representatives   judiciary

5. having to do with judges or courts of law

   judicial   independence   executive

6. the branch of government headed by the president. It sees that laws are carried out. Also, one who manages business affairs.

   executive   Senate   amendment

7. the written law and plan of a country's government

   Congress   Senate   constitution

8. freedom from control by another

   judicial   independence   delegate

9. a change or addition

   judiciary   executive   amendment

10. the part of the U.S. Constitution that defines basic rights and freedoms

    Bill of Rights   independence   Senate

Vocabulary: Meaning and Message © Fearon/Janus Publishers

Vocabulary Development: Proper Nouns

Name _____ Date _____

As you recall, a noun names a person, place, thing, event, or idea. How many nouns can you find in this sentence?

Joyce, the new student, introduced her father, Mr. Franklin, to her teacher, Ms. Anderson.

You may have noticed that the sentence includes six nouns: *Joyce, student, father, Mr. Franklin, teacher,* and *Ms. Anderson.* Do you notice any differences among the nouns? You might find it helpful to look at these in two separate columns:

student	Joyce
father	Mr. Franklin
teacher	Ms. Anderson

The nouns in the first column are called **common nouns.** A common noun refers to any person, place, thing, event, or idea. Some common nouns are *friend, city, mountain, concert,* and *hope.*

The nouns in the second column are **proper** nouns. A proper noun names a particular person, place, thing, event, or idea. Capitalize all proper nouns. Some proper nouns are *Fred, Ohio, American Medical Association,* and *Fourth of July.*

A. Here is a list of common nouns. After each one, write a proper noun that is a specific example of the common noun. The first one has been done for you.

1. **lake** _____*Lake Superior*_____

2. **street** _____

3. **nation** _____

4. **president** _____

5. **television show** _____

6. **movie star** _____

7. **friend** _____

8. **island** _____

9. **book** _____

10. **river** _____

Vocabulary: Meaning and Message © Fearon/Janus Publishers

Vocabulary Development: Proper Nouns

Name _____ Date _____

B. Here is a list of common nouns. Use each one in a sentence.

1. **amendment** _____

_____

2. **independence** _____

_____

3. **delegate** _____

_____

4. **country** _____

_____

5. **government** _____

_____

C. Here is a list of proper nouns. Use each one in a sentence.

1. **Congress** _____

_____

2. **Bill of Rights** _____

_____

3. **Constitution** _____

_____

4. **Supreme Court** _____

_____

5. **Senate** _____

_____

Vocabulary: Meaning and Message © Fearon/Janus Publishers

Puzzle

Name _____   Date _____

The words in the box can be found in the puzzle below. They may be written in any direction. Find and circle each one. You may want to check off each word in the box after you have circled it. One word has been circled and checked as an example.

bill of rights	judiciary	executive
representative	✔delegate senate	constitution
amendment	independent	congress

```
b i l l o f r i g h t s
r c v h h e j j e k n c
e q s d t g g t j j o o
p z d a g j a k l l i n
r w n r t g t u i i t s
e e e w e f g h j k u t
s f t l y o p a c b t i
e x e c u t i v e o i t
n d w e r t u i p p t u
t j u d i c i a r y s t
a m e n d m e n t p n i
t v o p n b h p o p o o
i n d e p e n d e n t n
v y y f v s w q o l m b
e b t e c o n g r e s s
```

Vocabulary: Meaning and Message © Fearon/Janus Publishers

Word Power: Pronouns

Name _____ Date _____

Read this paragraph. How does it sound to you?

Nicole picked up Nicole's jacket. Nicole put on Nicole's jacket. Nicole walked over to Nicole's friend Sam. Sam asked Nicole if Sam could walk Nicole home. Nicole said that Sam could.

You probably noticed that certain nouns were repeated over and over. Now read this paragraph and notice the differences.

Nicole picked up her jacket. She put it on. She walked over to her friend Sam. He asked Nicole if he could walk her home. She said that he could.

In the second paragraph, **pronouns** often replace the nouns *Nicole, sweater*, and *Sam*. A pronoun is a word that takes the place of one or more nouns.

Here are examples of the most commonly used pronouns:

I me you he she him her it we us they them

Some pronouns refer to persons, places, or things that are not specifically stated or known. These are called **indefinite pronouns.** Here's an example:

Someone took my jacket by mistake.

In that sentence, *someone* is the indefinite pronoun. Here are some other indefinite pronouns:

all anyone both everyone many most nobody somebody

Pronouns can also show ownership, or possession. These pronouns are called **possessive pronouns.** Here are some examples:

The seat by the window is *mine*. Where is *your* chair?

Here are some other possessive pronouns:

my mine your yours his her hers its
our ours your yours their theirs

Read each sentence. Underline regular pronouns once and indefinite pronouns twice. Circle each possessive pronoun.

1. "That hat is mine," she told him as he walked off with it.

2. Everyone saw them leave together.

3. Joe's mother told him she was glad he was home.

4. Someone left his or her bike there yesterday.

5. What will we do if nobody will help us move our car?

Writing on Your Own

Name _____ Date _____

Imagine that members of your local school board are thinking of writing rules about how students are to dress. Some students and parents feel that certain items of clothing shouldn't be worn to school. Some even want the students to wear uniforms. Others are opposed to all restrictions on what can and cannot be worn. How do you feel about this issue? Write a single general idea about any dress code you would like to see at your school.

_____

_____

Now write a list of rules that spell out just how you think students should dress.

_____

_____

_____

_____

_____

Why are you in favor of this plan? List as many ideas as you can think of.

_____

_____

_____

_____

_____

The school board is going to meet to discuss the issue. You plan to present your ideas at the meeting. Rewrite your ideas on a separate sheet of paper. Include the rules you would like to see followed. Tell why you think other plans are not as good as yours. Try to get the members of the school board to see things your way.

Vocabulary: Meaning and Message © Fearon/Janus Publishers

Lesson 1, Exercise 7
Test

Name _____ Date _____

Choose the best word or words to complete each sentence.

1. Women's right to vote is guaranteed by the 19th _____.

   A. judiciary   B. Senate   C. delegate   D. Amendment

2. Many countries have fought for _____ from unjust rule.

   A. independence   B. judicial   C. delegates   D. amend

3. The Constitution's first ten amendments form the _____.

   A. Bill of Rights   B. representative   C. Congress   D. Senate

4. Maria Jones is _____ in a sports company.

   A. an amendment   B. an executive   C. a judiciary   D. a constitution

5. The Supreme Court is part of the _____.

   A. independent   B. judiciary   C. Senate   D. amend

6. He was elected to be one of the two _____ from his state.

   A. courts   B. amendments   C. senators   D. execute

7. The House of _____ has 435 elected members.

   A. independent   B. jury   C. delegate   D. Representatives

8. Rosie knows what we need, so she should be our _____ at the next meeting.

   A. delegate   B. Senate   C. judiciary   D. amendment

9. All our state's basic laws are in our state's _____.

   A. constitution   B. executive   C. legal   D. independent

10. The Senate and the House of Representatives are the two parts of _____.

    A. delegate   B. Congress   C. amendment   D. Bill of Rights

Reading on Your Own

Name _____ Date _____

As you read this story, think about the meaning of each highlighted word.

The Industrial Revolution

Have you ever been in a **factory**? Factories produce goods quickly and in large numbers. The **mass production** of everything from television sets to bowling balls takes place in factories.

Less than 300 years ago, most products were made by hand. In the 1760s, however, machines were invented that could produce goods in one day that used to take weeks to make. Factories sprang up in big cities almost overnight. Workers rushed to the cities for the **opportunity** to work. This was known as the Industrial Revolution.

The center of the revolution was England. That country's **economy,** or system of managing wealth, changed greatly. London, the capital, experienced enormous **growth.** Unfortunately, some factory owners were greedy. To make as much money as they could, they cut costs in any way possible. Some provided shabby housing for their workers. Often several people lived in one tiny room. Many of these houses **lacked** fresh air and bathrooms. Disease was common. Women and children worked long hours. Factory owners liked to hire them because they worked for less money than men. Finally, in 1833, a law was passed in England that forbade very young children from working in factories. There were also laws that put **limits** on the hours women and children could work.

At this time in the United States, a system of **free enterprise** ruled. The government didn't get involved in private businesses. Here, too, factory owners often treated their workers unfairly. It wasn't until the early 20th century that workers began to unite. They formed labor unions to fight for better conditions.

Today, many people in unions think we are buying too many products from **foreign** countries. They feel that people in the United States should be buying more products that are made here. Many people also feel that a strong economy depends on **exporting,** or selling products outside our borders.

The struggle to protect workers is likely to continue.

What kind of factory would you like to visit? Why?

_____

_____

_____

Using Context

Name _____ Date _____

Circle the word that best completes each sentence.

1. Many products that are made in the United States are _____ to other countries.

   exported   lacked   factory   enterprise

2. Boring stories often _____ interesting characters.

   export   limit   lack   free

3. In rainy months, the grass's _____ is rapid.

   mass   limit   growth   export

4. Schools provide _____ for learning.

   enterprise   opportunities   produce   growth

5. He was arrested for driving faster than the speed _____.

   lack   limit   factory   economy

6. Automobiles are made in _____.

   limits   growth   economy   factories

7. I would love to travel and visit _____ countries.

   opportunity   factory   foreign   limited

8. In a healthy _____, few people are out of work.

   lack   factory   economy   limit

9. Private businesses decide how much goods will cost in a system of _____.

   factories   exports   limits   free enterprise

10. Automobiles can be quickly built, thanks to _____.

    mass production   free   economy   limit

Vocabulary Development: Homonyms

Name _____ Date _____

Do you know the difference between a *whale* and a *wail*? Do you know the difference between *turn* and *tern* or between *time* and *thyme*?

You probably know that a *whale* is a huge animal that lives in the sea and that a *wail* is a sorrowful cry. To *turn* is to twist or move in a circle. A *tern* is a kind of sea bird. *Time* is a period from the past to the future. *Thyme* is an herb used in cooking.

All these words have different meanings, but they also have something in common. Each pair is an example of **homonyms.** A homonym is a word that sounds the same as another word but means something else. Often, it is also spelled differently.

It's important to know the correct spellings of homonyms. If you don't, you might write something like this:

As Randy walked deeper into the forest, he heard a mysterious whale.

Most of your readers would wonder what a creature from the sea was doing in the middle of a forest!

Read the sets of homonyms below. Then use each word in a sentence of your own. If you aren't sure of a word's meaning, look it up in your dictionary.

1. **made** _____

   _____

   maid _____

   _____

2. **be** _____

   _____

   bee _____

   _____

3. **buy** _____

   _____

   by _____

   _____

Vocabulary: Meaning and Message © Fearon/Janus Publishers

Vocabulary Development: Homonyms

Name _____ Date _____

4. **new** _____

   _____

   knew _____

   _____

   gnu _____

   _____

5. **tale** _____

   _____

   tail _____

   _____

6. **one** _____

   _____

   won _____

   _____

7. **week** _____

   _____

   weak _____

   _____

8. **hire** _____

   _____

   higher _____

   _____

9. **ours** _____

   _____

   hours _____

   _____

Vocabulary: Meaning and Message © Fearon/Janus Publishers

Puzzle

Name _____ Date _____

Use the clues below to help you complete the puzzle. The answers can be found in the box.

> limit   lack   factory   production   export
> foreign   enterprise   growth   opportunity   economy

Across
3. how resources are managed
5. from another place
6. manufacturing
7. the opposite of *shrinking*
8. boundary

Down
1. a place where goods are produced
2. to send goods to another country to be sold there
3. business
4. possibility
8. to not have

Word Power: Verbs

Name _____ Date _____

If you've ever listened to a basketball game on the radio, you've probably heard something like this:

He *races* down the court and *heads* for the basket. He *passes* the ball to the forward, who *leaps* high in the air and *shoots*.

Sportscasters try to make what they see as exciting as they can for their listeners. One way they do this is by using words that paint sharp mental pictures. **Verbs** can do this. A verb is a word that expresses action or state of being.

Action Verbs: catch, swim, dance, sing, throw, leap

The verbs above show *physical* action. *Mental* action is shown by verbs such as these: hope, want, think, imagine.

State-of-Being Verbs: is, are, was, were, am, will be

Verbs can also show tense, or the time when the action or state of being happens. The three tenses used most often are present, past, and future.

Present Tense:	arrive	borrow	learn
Past Tense:	arrived	borrowed	learned
Future Tense:	will (shall) arrive	will (shall) borrow	will (shall) learn

As you can see, the past tense of these verbs is formed by adding *d* or *ed* to the present tense. *Irregular* verbs, however, do not form their past tense in this way. For example, the past tense of *teach* is *taught*. The past tense of *sit* is *sat*. A dictionary will give you the past tense of all irregular verbs.

Complete these sentences with the past tense of the highlighted verbs. The first three are formed by adding *d* or *ed* to the present tense. The last three are irregular. If you do not know their past tense forms, look them up in a dictionary.

1. **pick**   Lou _____ some flowers.

2. **help**   Samantha _____ her mother wash the car.

3. **explain**   The teacher _____ the lesson.

4. **find**   Al _____ a dollar on the sidewalk.

5. **make**   Nadia _____ lunch for us.

6. **do**   Tina _____ her homework this morning.

Vocabulary: Meaning and Message © Fearon/Janus Publishers

Writing on Your Own

Name _____ Date _____

Imagine yourself owning a factory. You want your employees'
working conditions to be the best that you can make them.
Answer these questions to tell how you would do this.
How many hours a day would your employees work? How
much would they be paid per hour?

_____

How many vacation days per year should your employees
have? Should this number be the same for all? Explain.

_____

_____

Would your factory provide day care for employees' children?
Why?

_____

_____

Some people think workplaces should have sports facilities,
such as gyms that the workers can use. Do you? Why?

_____

_____

_____

Now imagine that you are a worker in a factory. You like your
job a lot. Why are you glad to be working where you are?

_____

_____

_____

_____

_____

_____

Vocabulary: Meaning and Message © Fearon/Janus Publishers

Lesson 2, Exercise 7
Test

Name _____ Date _____

Choose the word that is being described.

1. to sell goods to other countries

    A. export   B. free enterprise   C. mass production   D. lack

2. to be without or to not have enough

    A. export   B. mass production   C. lack   D. economy

3. increase; development

    A. opportunity   B. foreign   C. growth   D. factory

4. the point at which something ends; the greatest number allowed

    A. lack   B. limit   C. opportunity   D. growth

5. a place where products are made

    A. mass production   B. factory   C. export   D. foreign

6. the way a country produces, distributes, and uses its wealth and resources

    A. growth   B. opportunity   C. factory   D. economy

7. the making of large quantities of products, usually with machines and by several people working on one product, each doing a separate task

    A. free enterprise   B. opportunity   C. mass production   D. lack

8. a system in which private businesses are under little government control. They decide for themselves how they will produce and sell goods. They set their own prices.

    A. export   B. mass production   C. free enterprise   D. economy

9. a good chance; the right time to do something

    A. limit   B. export   C. free enterprise   D. opportunity

10. of, from, or concerning another country

    A. foreign   B. mass production   C. free enterprise   D. growth

Reading on Your Own

Name _____ Date _____

As you read this story, think about the meaning of each highlighted word.

The Melting Pot

Do you know where your **ancestors** came from? Were your grandparents and great-grandparents born here or in another country? The United States has been called a "melting pot" of different **cultures.** People of native American, European, African, Asian, Hispanic and other backgrounds call this country home.

About 500 years ago, in the 15th **century,** people started **emigrating** from, or leaving, Europe to live in North and South America. Many of them were looking for riches. Some were looking for freedom. Others wanted to own land or earn a better living.

Some people were forced to leave their homelands. Millions of people came to North and South America from Africa. They were brought as slaves.

By the 1890s, millions of **immigrants**, or people who have come to live in a new country, were arriving in the United States every year. Many of these people were European **peasants** who had worked on small farms. A great number of them arrived here on steamships that stopped at Ellis Island in New York Harbor. Here the immigrants were interviewed and checked for diseases. Health laws were strictly **enforced.** Anyone who had a disease that others could catch was sent home. Recently, the Ellis Island immigration center was restored. It is now a popular tourist attraction.

The movement of large **groups** of people has continued. Recent wars have forced millions of people to leave their homes in Southeast Asia, Central America, and the Middle East. Many of these people have moved to the United States. Many people have also come here from poor countries in order to escape **poverty** and to find work that will support them. Like the immigrants of the past, these people have made our **society** richer. America's mix of individuals and groups, with their different skills and talents, is one of our greatest sources of strength.

What three things would you like to know about your ancestors?

_____

_____

_____

Vocabulary: Meaning and Message © Fearon/Janus Publishers

Using Context

Name _____ Date _____

Circle the word that is being described.

1. to leave one country and go to live in another

   immigrant   enforce   emigrate

2. one hundred years

   poverty   emigration   century

3. your family members who lived before you

   ancestors   societies   peasants

4. to bring about by force; to make sure people obey something, such as a law

   emigrate   enforce   peasant

5. one who comes into a new country

   immigrant   peasant   group

6. a condition of having very little money

   society   ancestor   poverty

7. a person who works on a small farm

   group   peasant   ancestor

8. people or things that are together

   ancestors   immigrants   group

9. people with similar ways of living who form a group; all people

   peasants   society   ancestors

10. the way of life of a group of people—how they think and act

    culture   poverty   enforcement

Vocabulary: Meaning and Message © Fearon/Janus Publishers

Vocabulary Development: Word Families

Name _____ Date _____

Have you ever been told that you look like someone in your family? Maybe your eyes are like your father's eyes or your hair looks like your mother's. You may have an uncle's mouth or a grandmother's nose.

People in families often resemble, or look like, each other. However, each person is an individual. In a similar way, words can resemble each other. Do you see the similarities and differences in these words?

form   reform   formula   formation   formality
format   formative   form letter   formulate

Creating words from other words can be fun. You and your friends might even make a game of it. For example, by adding the letters *in* to the word *form*, you get the word *inform*. Can you think of any words that resemble *this* new word?

Add letters or syllables to *hand* to see how many new words you can come up with. Here are a few to get you started: *handle, hand-to-hand,* and *handout.*

Many of the words below are from the same "word family." Use each in a separate sentence. If you are unsure of a word's meaning, look it up in a dictionary.

1. **ancestor** _____

   _____

   ancestral _____

   _____

2. **culture** _____

   _____

   cultural _____

   _____

   culture shock _____

   _____

Vocabulary: Meaning and Message © Fearon/Janus Publishers

Vocabulary Development: Word Families

Name _____ Date _____

3. **migrate** _____

_____

emigrate _____

_____

emigrant _____

_____

immigrant _____

_____

immigration _____

_____

4. **enforce** _____

_____

forceful _____

_____

5. **group** _____

_____

regroup _____

_____

6. **cycle** _____

_____

bicycle _____

_____

cyclical _____

_____

Vocabulary: Meaning and Message © Fearon/Janus Publishers

Puzzle

Name _____ Date _____

Choose a word from the box that fits each description.

ancestors	century	culture	emigrate	enforce
group	immigrate	peasant	poverty	society

1. to move from one's country ___ ◯ ___ ___ ___ ___ ___ ___

2. a farmer ___ ◯ ___ ___ ___ ___ ___

3. how people live ___ ___ ◯ ___ ___ ___ ___

4. ten decades ___ ___ ◯ ___ ___ ___ ___

5. to move into a country ___ ___ ___ ◯ ___ ___ ___ ___

6. to see that a law is followed ___ ◯ ___ ___ ___ ___ ___

7. a collection of people ◯ ___ ___ ___ ___

8. the condition of being poor ◯ ___ ___ ___ ___ ___ ___

9. everyone as a group ___ ◯ ___ ___ ___ ___ ___

10. the people from whom one is descended

    ___ ___ ___ ___ ___ ◯ ___ ___ ___

To solve this puzzle, write the circled letters in order on the lines below. The words offer one description of the United States.

___ ___ ___ ___ ___ ___ ___   ___ ___ ___

Lesson 3, Exercise 5
Word Power: Adjectives

Name _____ Date _____

Are you *shy, outgoing, quiet, talkative, short, tall, kind, generous, funny,* or *lovable*? Is your bedroom *small, large, crowded, messy, clean,* or *dark*? All these italicized words are *adjectives*. They are used to describe people, places, and things.

Adjectives help you create clearer pictures of what you are speaking or writing about. For example, if you say the word *shoe*, a picture of a shoe will form in your listener's mind. You can make that picture clearer if you use adjectives such as *brown, shiny, scuffed, suede,* or *expensive.* Try to create as clear and vivid a picture of your thoughts as you can.

Adjectives can describe various qualities, such as size, color, and texture. They can also tell "which one" or "how many." Here are some examples of adjectives describing nouns:

large room　　**purple** tie　　**rough** cloth　　**those** players　　**seven** tables

Adjectives are used in comparisons. For example, you may be *tall,* but your brother may be *taller,* and your sister *tallest.* You may be *careful,* but a friend may be *more careful* and your cousin the *most careful.*

As you can see, there are two ways to form comparisons with adjectives. One is to add *er* or *est* to the end of the adjective. The other is to add the word *more* or *most* before the adjective. Adjectives of one syllable take the endings *er* and *est.* Adjectives with three or more syllables use the words *more* and *most.* The method for adjectives with two syllables varies. Here are some examples:

One syllable:	kind	kinder	kindest
Two syllables:	heavy	heavier	heaviest
	famous	more famous	most famous
Three syllables:	beautiful	more beautiful	most beautiful

Complete these sentences with adjectives.

1. Stu planted flowers in his _____ backyard.

2. _____ children are playing on the

   _____ floor.

3. Hank is _____ .

4. Janine is _____ than Hank.

5. Paula is _____ of all.

Vocabulary: Meaning and Message © Fearon/Janus Publishers

Writing on Your Own

Name _____ Date _____

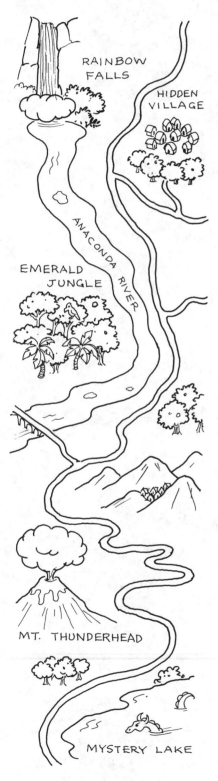

RAINBOW FALLS

HIDDEN VILLAGE

ANACONDA RIVER

EMERALD JUNGLE

MT. THUNDERHEAD

MYSTERY LAKE

Suppose you are going to move to a foreign country. Which country would it be? List two countries you might like to move to, if only for a very short time.

_____

For each country you listed, tell why that country is of interest to you. Is it the weather, the geography, or the scenery? Do you know people who live there? Is there a certain kind of lifestyle you like there?

_____

_____

_____

_____

_____

People who move to other countries often have to adjust to new conditions. For instance, they might have to learn new languages or eat different foods. How might your life in the countries you listed be different from your life here? How would you have to change?

_____

_____

_____

_____

_____

Now suppose that you can either move or stay here. Which would you choose? Why?

_____

_____

Vocabulary: Meaning and Message © Fearon/Janus Publishers

Test

Name _____ Date _____

Choose the best word to complete each sentence.

1. We returned to the town in Mexico where my _____ lived.

   A. century   B. emigration   C. immigrant   D. ancestors

2. The first year of the 20th _____ was 1901.

   A. century   B. emigration   C. poverty   D. group

3. I am a recent _____ to this country.

   A. group   B. ancestor   C. society   D. immigrant

4. I _____ from Canada.

   A. enforced   B. emigrated   C. immigrant   D. ancestors

5. After the accident, driving regulations were more strictly _____.

   A. ignored   B. immigrated   C. enforced   D. ancestral

6. It is a rich country, but some people live in great _____.

   A. poverty   B. immigration   C. peasants   D. centuries

7. Although they worked long hours in the field, the _____ earned little money.

   A. emigrations   B. ancestors   C. groups   D. peasants

8. Gather together in _____ of three.

   A. groups   B. cultures   C. societies   D. peasants

9. Governments should work to serve _____.

   A. emigrate   B. century   C. society   D. poverty

10. Korean _____ is very interesting.

    A. enforcement   B. culture   C. century   D. immigrants

Vocabulary: Meaning and Message © Fearon/Janus Publishers

Reading on Your Own

Name _____ Date _____

As you read this story, think about the meaning of each highlighted word.

Save the Planet

In the 18th century, during the Industrial Revolution, thick black factory smoke filled the air of American cities. At the time, most people thought very little of the **environment.** They didn't realize the serious damage that can result from dirtying our air, water, and land.

Pollution can be caused by smoke, garbage, chemicals, waste products, and automobile exhaust fumes. Today, many people feel that it is our **duty** to preserve the environment. If we don't, then the **generations** to come, including our own children and grandchildren, could suffer greatly.

The relationship between living beings and their natural environment is called "ecology." The ecology **movement** is said to have started in the late 1960s. Then, people began to become aware of the many ways in which we can harm our planet. Rachel Carson is sometimes called the "founder" of this movement. In 1962, she wrote a book called *Silent Spring.* It warned of the dangers of insecticides. These chemicals are sprayed on crops to kill bugs. Carson warned that the chemicals can also be harmful to people.

Organizations such as the Sierra Club have been formed to protect the environment. Among other things, the members of these groups work to save **wilderness** areas and have **opposed** the killing of endangered species. They want the government to keep forest lands from being destroyed. They want to stop the disappearance of various kinds of plants and animals.

We can all find ways to show our respect for the earth. We can **recycle,** or reuse, things like paper, plastic, and glass. We can walk more and drive less. We can turn off electric lights we're not using. We can study **petitions** that ask for laws that will help keep the environment healthy. We can increase our own **knowledge** of the situation. By becoming better informed, we will be better able to make the future what we wish it to be.

What might your class be able to do as a group to clean up a dirty environment?

_____

_____

_____

Vocabulary: Meaning and Message © Fearon/Janus Publishers

Using Context

Name _____ Date _____

Read each sentence below. Then choose a word from the box to replace the highlighted words. Write the word on the line.

duty	environment	generations
movement	oppose	polluted	recycled
wilderness	petition	knowledge

1. We wrote a **formal request** to get city taxes lowered.

   _____

2. Fish can't live in **dirtied** rivers. _____

3. Different **groups of people in family history** see things differently. _____

4. My **understanding** of your language is limited.

   _____

5. Our **surroundings** changed when we moved.

   _____

6. Paper, glass, and plastic can all be **used again.**

   _____

7. Chuck likes to hike in the **place where no people live.**

   _____

8. If you work, it is your **responsibility** to pay taxes.

   _____

9. Henry wants to drive, but his parents **are against** the idea.

   _____

10. We are involved in an **organized group effort** to help save our national forests. _____

Vocabulary Development: Analogies

Name _____ Date _____

Imagine that you've seen a new movie. When telling a friend about it, this is what you say:

> The story was like *Star Wars,* but it was less exciting. The ending reminded me of *Back to the Future.* The characters were a little bit like those in *E.T.*

Describing something by comparing it to something else is a common way of making one's ideas clear. These kinds of comparisons are called **analogies.**

In school, you may come across analogies on test questions. The questions ask you to find the relationships between words. For example:

Cloud is to *sky* as *tree* is to _____.

a. ocean   b. land   c. birds   d. sun

To answer this question, you first have to ask yourself what the relationship is between a cloud and the sky. Clouds are found in the sky. Now look at the word *tree.* Try to find the same relationship between the word *tree* and one of the four possible answers. Ask yourself, "Which word tells where a tree can be found?" The answer is "land."

Here are some of the ways in which words that are used in analogies can be related to each other:

Words can be synonyms. They can have the same or nearly the same meanings:

> *yell* is to *scream*

Words can be antonyms. They can have opposite meanings:

> *bored* is to *excited*

One word can tell what another word does:

> *bake* is to *chef*

One word can be a category of another word:

> *ballet* is to *dance*

Circle the letter beside the word that completes the analogy.

1. **Opposed** is to **against** as **new** is to _____.

    a. old   b. modern   c. ruined   c. destroy

2. **Polluted** is to **pure** as **fast** is to _____.

    a. quick   b. speedy   c. run   d. slow

Vocabulary Development: Analogies

Name _____ Date _____

3. **Duty** is to **responsibility** as **search** is to _____.

   a. misplace   b. treasure   c. seek   d. secret

4. **Environment** is to **surroundings** as **put** is to _____.

   a. take   b. place   c. abandon   d. sit

5. **Wilderness** is to **city** as **warm** is to _____.

   a. summer   b. temperature   c. heat   d. cool

6. **Movement** is to **motion** as **bother** is to _____.

   a. love   b. like   c. annoy   d. sister

7. **Tall** is to **short** as **win** is to _____.

   a. succeed   b. travel   c. lose   d. basketball

8. **Hard** is to **soft** as **dry** is to _____.

   a. wonderful   b. towel   c. wet   d. desert

9. **South Dakota** is to **state** as **Paris** is to _____.

   a. river   b. France   c. city   d. large

10. **Heals** is to **doctor** as **writes** is to _____.

    a. butcher   b. book   c. author   d. typewriter

11. **School** is to **student** as **hospital** is to _____.

    a. sick   b. white   c. medicine   d. patient

12. **Respect** is to **admire** as **jolly** is to _____.

    a. angry   b. target   c. merry   d. anxious

13. **Purr** is to **cat** as **bark** is to _____.

    a. dog   b. clown   c. animal   d. bird

14. **Los Angeles Lakers** is to **team** as **oak** is to _____.

    a. leaf   b. trunk   c. tree   d. maple

Puzzle

Name _____ Date _____

Unscramble the highlighted letters in each sentence to form a word from the box. Write the word on the line.

environment   duty   generation
knowledge   petition   movement
oppose   pollution   recycle   wilderness

1. Keeping the pool clean is the lifeguard's **t u d y.**

   _____

2. Burning garbage can cause air **l i p t o n o u l.**

   _____

3. I favor what you **s o p e p o.** _____

4. Sixties rock is the music of my parents' **n a r e g i t o n e.**

   _____

5. Their reform **m e n t o m e v** became popular.

   _____

6. Her warmth and good humor create a cheerful
   n n e i v o r e n m t. _____

7. We **y c l r c e e** what can still be used.

   _____

8. We live ten miles from town, surrounded by **s e n e l i d s r w.**

   _____

9. Our **t o n p i i t e** was addressed to the city council.

   _____

10. One way to gain **w o n g e l d e k** is to ask questions.

    _____

Vocabulary: Meaning and Message © Fearon/Janus Publishers

Word Power: Adverbs

Name _____ Date _____

What do the italicized words in these sentences have in common?

Wendy drives *carefully*.
Frank speaks *loudly*.
Victor skates *beautifully*.

All the italicized words tell how someone *does* something. They all describe the verbs in their sentences. Words that describe verbs are called **adverbs.** Adverbs can also describe adjectives or other adverbs. Here are some examples of each of these three uses of adverbs. The adverbs are highlighted. The words they describe are in italics.

Adverbs describing verbs:

Kim *sings* **magnificently.**   Taylor *eats* **hungrily.**
Nancy *works* **slowly.**

Adverbs describing adjectives:

Georgia is **quite** *late*.   She is **extremely** *kind*.
That music is **too** *noisy*.

Adverbs describing adverbs:

Jamal sings **very** *softly*.   Ned ate **so** *quietly*.
The day went **quite** *smoothly*.

Adverbs, like adjectives, can be used in comparisons. Here are some examples:

Tim eats *slowly*.   Yolanda works *happily*.
Carla eats *more slowly*.   Ed works *less happily*.
Betty eats the *most slowly* of all.   Keith works the *least happily* of all.

Complete each sentence by adding an adverb.

1. Todd looked _____ happy.

2. Wendy danced _____ joyfully.

3. The bus lurched _____ across town.

4. He complained _____.

5. I entered the building _____.

6. It was a _____ exciting movie.

7. The dog was _____ tired to move.

Writing on Your Own

Name _____ Date _____

Have you ever seen or heard the slogan Save the Whales? It is used by people who know that if certain kinds of whales are not protected, those species may disappear.

Slogans are used by individuals and groups to express ideas they believe in. The ideas may be about the environment or about any other issue of concern.

Here's a chance to express your views. Write a slogan that shows how you feel about an issue you think is important. Try writing several until you are satisfied with one. Good slogans are usually short and catchy.

_____

_____

_____

_____

_____

How can the slogan be used? Where could it appear?

_____

_____

_____

_____

_____

_____

Imagine that your slogan is going to be used on a bumper sticker. On a separate sheet of paper, design the bumper sticker. Use any colors, lettering, and shapes or figures that you wish.

Vocabulary: Meaning and Message © Fearon/Janus Publishers

Test

Name _____ Date _____

Choose the best word to complete each sentence.

1. When I learned to read, my _____ increased greatly.

   A. duty   B. movement   C. wilderness   D. knowledge

2. That car wash uses _____ water.

   A. recycled   B. petition   C. pollute   D. oppose

3. An oil spill _____ the bay.

   A. petition   B. polluted   C. environment   D. generations

4. I signed a _____ asking for better after-school sports programs.

   A. wilderness   B. pollution   C. duty   D. petition

5. Julia created a different _____ in every room.

   A. generation   B. environment   C. movement   D. duty

6. People with different ideas _____ our movement.

   A. opposed   B. polluted   C. petitioned   D. generations

7. Our grandparents were born two _____ ago.

   A. movement   B. wilderness   C. pollution   D. generations

8. Do bears in the zoo remember the _____?

   A. wilderness   B. recycles   C. petitions   D. pollution

9. The civil rights _____ led to the passage of the Voting Rights Act.

   A. generation   B. wilderness   C. movement   D. duty

10. My new job included new _____.

    A. movement   B. pollution   C. petition   D. duties

Unit 3 Review

Name _____ Date _____

A. Choose the word or phrase that means about the same as the highlighted word. Darken the circled letter.

1. **century**
   - Ⓐ one hundred years
   - Ⓑ society
   - Ⓒ generation
   - Ⓓ growth

2. **group**
   - Ⓐ ancestor
   - Ⓑ immigrant
   - Ⓒ gathering
   - Ⓓ peasant

3. **opposed**
   - Ⓐ enforced
   - Ⓑ against
   - Ⓒ limited
   - Ⓓ lack

4. **lack**
   - Ⓐ pollution
   - Ⓑ opportunity
   - Ⓒ export
   - Ⓓ want

5. **reuse**
   - Ⓐ recycle
   - Ⓑ pollution
   - Ⓒ environment
   - Ⓓ movement

6. **duty**
   - Ⓐ factory
   - Ⓑ responsibility
   - Ⓒ petition
   - Ⓓ economy

7. **knowledge**
   - Ⓐ production
   - Ⓑ wilderness
   - Ⓒ emigration
   - Ⓓ understanding

8. **opportunity**
   - Ⓐ chance
   - Ⓑ foreign
   - Ⓒ duty
   - Ⓓ poverty

9. **enterprise**
   - Ⓐ business
   - Ⓑ economy
   - Ⓒ pollution
   - Ⓓ peasant

10. **emigrate**
    - Ⓐ foreign
    - Ⓑ immigrant
    - Ⓒ leave
    - Ⓓ ancestors

11. **customs**
    - Ⓐ century
    - Ⓑ culture
    - Ⓒ opportunity
    - Ⓓ movement

12. **pollute**
    - Ⓐ environment
    - Ⓑ factory
    - Ⓒ society
    - Ⓓ dirty

13. **export**
    - Ⓐ enterprise
    - Ⓑ sell to another country
    - Ⓒ produce
    - Ⓓ culture

Vocabulary: Meaning and Message © Fearon/Janus Publishers

Unit 3 Review

Name _____ Date _____

B. Darken the circled letter beside the word that is being described.

1. to see that a law is followed
   - (A) export
   - (B) enforce
   - (C) oppose
   - (D) pollute

2. organized group effort
   - (A) movement
   - (B) emergency
   - (C) measurement
   - (D) vary

3. unexplored land
   - (A) between
   - (B) immigrant
   - (C) wilderness
   - (D) balance

4. increase
   - (A) fewer
   - (B) less
   - (C) inquire
   - (D) growth

5. freedom
   - (A) independence
   - (B) endorse
   - (C) manage
   - (D) loan

6. Senate and House
   - (A) interest
   - (B) Congress
   - (C) Constitution
   - (D) finance

7. manager
   - (A) details
   - (B) economic
   - (C) executive
   - (D) growth

8. person who acts for others
   - (A) average
   - (B) interest
   - (C) ancestor
   - (D) delegate

9. change or addition
   - (A) calculate
   - (B) foreign
   - (C) amendment
   - (D) judiciary

10. lack of money
   - (A) generation
   - (B) poverty
   - (C) society
   - (D) limit

11. farm worker
   - (A) peasant
   - (B) economy
   - (C) petition
   - (D) finance

12. to move into a country
   - (A) judiciary
   - (B) environment
   - (C) immigrate
   - (D) Bill of Rights

13. to make things in large numbers, usually by machine
   - (A) measure
   - (B) agree
   - (C) mortgage
   - (D) mass produce

Reading on Your Own

Name _____ Date _____

As you read this story, think about the meaning of each highlighted word.

Jackie!

Jackie Joyner-Kersee has been called the world's greatest female athlete. She has broken many **track** records and has won two Olympic gold medals.

Jackie was born in 1962 in East St. Louis, Illinois. At an early age, she showed a love of running. When she was only 12, Jackie was practicing the long jump. At that age, she was able to jump 16 feet, 9 inches! In high school, she was captain of her volleyball team. She also starred in basketball and track.

In 1980, Jackie's athletic abilities helped her win a scholarship to the University of California in Los Angeles. In 1986, she received the Sullivan Award. This award is given to the best U.S. amateur athlete.

Many people regard Jackie's husband, Bob Kersee, as one of the reasons behind her success. As Jackie practices, Bob watches her performance carefully and then offers **guidance.** Jackie is a good **listener.** She pays attention to the criticism as well as the support. **Together,** Jackie and Bob are a good team.

Jackie is strong, graceful, and hard-working. Other athletes **speak** with admiration about how serious she is. During track **season,** she controls what she eats, gets plenty of sleep, and practices as often as she can.

At the 1988 Summer Olympics in Seoul, South Korea, Jackie received two **separate** gold medals. One was for the long jump and the other for the women's heptathlon. The heptathlon is made up of seven different events. They are 100-meter hurdles, shot-put, javelin throw, high jump, long jump, 200-meter run, and 800-meter run. The gold medal is given to the **person** who scores the highest number of points in the seven events. In 1988, Jackie scored nearly 2,000 points more than her closest rival! In a way, though, it wasn't much of a **surprise.** Many people **concede** that Jackie Joyner-Kersee is one of the finest athletes the world has ever seen.

Which sport do you most like to watch? Why?

_____

_____

_____

Vocabulary: Meaning and Message © Fearon/Janus Publishers

Lesson 1, Exercise 2
Using Context

Name _____ Date _____

Circle the word that is being described.

1. a human being; a man, woman, or child

   listener   person   surprise

2. something unexpected that occurs, making one feel amazement or wonder

   concede   season   surprise

3. to talk; to utter words

   speak   concede   surprise

4. athletic events that take place on a running course; a trail, path, or course

   separate   track   guidance

5. a person who pays attention to what others say

   listener   speak   season

6. to admit as true; to recognize; to admit defeat in an election

   surprise   concede   guidance

7. the time when something takes place; spring, summer, fall, or winter

   speak   season   track

8. the act of guiding, leading, or directing

   listener   season   guidance

9. with another or others; in one place; at one time

   separate   together   surprise

10. apart; divided

    together   separate   concede

Vocabulary Development: Idioms

Name _____ Date _____

Here's an old joke:

Tommy: Did you take a bath today?
Randy: Why? Is one missing?

The humor of this joke depends on the use of an **idiom.** An idiom is a phrase whose meaning is different from the usual meaning of the words in the phrase. When you say, *take* a bath, you're not really talking about removing it. However, the use of the phrase "take a bath" is so common that we forget it doesn't mean exactly what it says.

Every language has its own idioms. The English language is full of them. Here are some examples:

"The bank was *held up* yesterday." (Thieves didn't actually hold the bank over their heads. In this case, "to hold up" means "to rob at gunpoint.")

"Will you stop *picking on* your little brother?" (No one is actually choosing anyone else. *"To pick on"* means "to pester" or "to annoy.")

People who are learning a new language can find idioms very confusing. For example, imagine that someone who is learning English hears this: "He was just pulling my leg." The phrase "pulling my leg" means "fooling" or "joking with." If you were hearing it for the first time, you might wonder why someone had been yanking someone else's leg.

Here are some idioms and their definitions. Each idiom is used in a sentence as an example. You'll recognize some of the words in the idioms. They appeared in the story on page 106. Use each idiom in a sentence of your own.

1. **in person**—physically present
Jane Fonda appeared in person at our shopping mall.

_____

_____

2. **put up with**—endure
I can't put up with this noise.

_____

_____

Vocabulary Development: Idioms

Name _____ Date _____

3. **rule out**—eliminate
We can't rule out the possibility that it will rain tonight.

_____

_____

4. **speak out**—to say what's on one's mind
It's time that we spoke out about the traffic problem in this town.

_____

_____

5. **in regard to**—about
This letter is in regard to our conversation yesterday.

_____

_____

6. **in season**—at the best time for eating; ripe
Peaches are in season during most of the summer.

_____

_____

7. **speak up**—to speak loudly and clearly enough to be understood
Please speak up so the people in the back row can hear you.

_____

_____

8. **see through**—to understand the truth of something
The principal saw through Vince's excuses right away.

_____

_____

9. **beside the point**—having no importance to the matter
It is beside the point to discuss the prom while debating the school lunch program.

_____

_____

Puzzle

Name _____ Date _____

Use the clues to help you complete the crossword puzzle. The answers can be found in the box.

speak	together	listen	season	guidance
separate	concede	person	surprise	track

Across
2. running events
3. standing alone
5. a member of the human race
6. leadership
8. winter, for example

Down
1. to say
2. joined
3. a shocker
4. acknowledge
7. to pay attention

Lesson 1, Exercise 5

Word Power: Prepositions

Name _____ Date _____

Did you ever sing, "When you wish below a star"? or "Somewhere under the rainbow"? Have you ever read the book *The Adventures Without Huckleberry Finn*?

Does something seem strange about any of the words above? One word in each song or book title has been changed. The words that don't belong are the **prepositions** *below, under,* and *without.* A preposition shows how a noun or pronoun and another word or group of words are related. Prepositions are often small words, but they can make a big difference in what the words around them mean.

In each example above, the relationship shown by the preposition is incorrect. The words to the first song are, "When you wish *upon* a star," not *below* a star. You would sing, "Somewhere *over* the rainbow," not *under* the rainbow. The book is called *The Adventures* of *Huckleberry Finn*, not *without* Huckleberry Finn.

Use each of the prepositions below in a sentence of your own.

1. **without** _____

   _____

2. **since** _____

   _____

3. **during** _____

   _____

4. **among** _____

   _____

5. **toward** _____

   _____

6. **within** _____

   _____

Vocabulary: Meaning and Message © Fearon/Janus Publishers

Writing on Your Own

Name _____ Date _____

Suppose you could be a famous sports star. You might be a high-scoring basketball player. You could be an Olympic ice-skating champion. What kind of sports star would you like to be?

_____

What do you imagine you would have to do in order to become that star? Include as many details as possible. For instance, you might have to practice ice-skating for four hours every day for the next ten years. You might also have to take ballet lessons.

_____

_____

_____

_____

_____

What do you think life is like for sports stars? Jot down your ideas about how they spend their days. Include the good and the bad parts of this way of life.

_____

_____

_____

_____

_____

_____

_____

_____

_____

Vocabulary: Meaning and Message © Fearon/Janus Publishers

Lesson 1, Exercise 7
Test

Name _____ Date _____

Choose the best word to complete each sentence.

1. We argued for hours, but I finally had to _____ that you were right.

   A. listener   B. concede   C. track   D. spoke

2. Of all my friends, Della is the _____ I admire most.

   A. person   B. listener   C. concede   D. season

3. Uri paid close attention and was praised for being a good _____.

   A. surprise   B. listener   C. guidance   D. track

4. He was so _____ he couldn't say a word.

   A. separate   B. conceded   C. together   D. surprised

5. After the argument, they stopped _____ to each other.

   A. track   B. speaking   C. separate   D. guide

6. Summer is Rhoda's favorite _____.

   A. surprise   B. guidance   C. listener   D. season

7. The school's best athletes ran around the _____.

   A. concede   B. surprise   C. track   D. season

8. Tanya loves her dog. The two can always be seen _____.

   A. separate   B. surprise   C. together   D. track

9. In the library, there is a _____ room for magazines.

   A. separate   B. together   C. listener   D. speak

10. Can you tell me where to go? I need your _____.

    A. track   B. season   C. guidance   D. surprise

Reading on Your Own

Name _____ Date _____

As you read this story, think about the meaning of each highlighted word.

Basketball

Baseball is played mostly in North America, Latin America, and Japan. Soccer is popular in Europe and South America. Basketball, however, is played around the world. It is often considered the "international game."

Basketball was invented by James Naismith in 1891. Naismith was a teacher at a school in Massachusetts. He combined the native American game of lacrosse with the British game of soccer. In the new game, team members bounced, or "dribbled," the ball and tried to throw it into one of a pair of peach baskets. The **angle** at which they tossed it had to be just right. If they put the ball in a basket, they'd score two points. The opposing team, **dispersed** around the court, tried to prevent them from doing this. Every so often, a **collision** would take place when two players bumped into one another. Generally speaking, however, the players were injured less often than they were in lacrosse and soccer games.

During World War I, many Americans were sent to Europe to fight. Some took the game of basketball with them. Basketball's **ascent** to widespread popularity soon followed. In time, it **emerged** as a professional sport. Today young people throughout the country can dream of **pursuing** careers in the game.

The rules have changed a bit since Naismith's day. Because he had 18 boys in his class, Naismith divided them into two teams of nine members each. In today's game, there are five players on each side.

Basketball is fast-paced and exciting. Players **expend** a great deal of energy running up and down the court and making **incredible** shots. They are **adept** at shooting from almost any spot. As the minutes and seconds of the game **elapse,** the fans cheer for the players. It is interesting to wonder whether James Naismith ever imagined how exciting his game would turn out to be.

What is your favorite sport? Explain why you like it so much.

_____

_____

_____

Vocabulary: Meaning and Message © Fearon/Janus Publishers

Lesson 2, Exercise 2
Using Context

Name _____ Date _____

Circle the word that is being described.

1. a crash; a sudden violent coming together

   adept   angle   collision

2. very good at something; expert; highly skilled

   ascent   adept   incredible

3. the act of going up or rising; the act of moving up in rank
   or fame

   ascent   angle   expend

4. the shape that is formed when two straight lines meet at a point

   angle   ascent   elapse

5. to pass or slip by, usually said of time

   disperse   emerge   elapse

6. to break up and scatter in all directions; to distribute widely

   emerge   disperse   ascent

7. to come into view; to become apparent or known

   pursue   elapse   emerge

8. to spend; to use up

   incredible   expend   ascent

9. unbelievable; amazing; not credible

   incredible   dispersed   angle

10. to follow in order to catch up with; to follow a plan

    pursue   disperse   ascent

Vocabulary Development: Confusing Words

Name _____ Date _____

Imagine this. Two bowls are side by side. One has sugar in it, the other salt. You are going to put your spoon in one and sprinkle the contents on your cereal. Do you think you can pick the bowl that has the sugar in it?

Sugar and salt aren't the only things that can look alike and cause confusion. Words, too, often look like other words. However, they may have different meanings and slightly different spellings. For instance, look at the words *formerly* and *formally* in the sentences below:

Our football coach was *formerly* the science teacher.
The diplomas were *formally* handed to the new graduates.

The italicized words sound almost the same, but they are spelled differently, and they have different meanings. The word *formerly* means "at an earlier, or former, time." The word *formally* means "done in an official, or formal, way."

Knowing the differences between words that are easily confused will help you understand what you read and hear. It will also help you when you want to be understood by others. It is especially important when you are writing. Using the wrong word can confuse your readers. If they get too confused, they might just stop reading. Of course this is not what you want them to do, especially when you have something important to tell them.

Here are some groups of words that often cause confusion. Read each word and its definition. Then use the word in a sentence of your own. If you need help, look up the word in a dictionary.

1. **adept**—skillful; talented

   _____

   _____

   adopt—to become a parent to; to take up as one's own

   _____

   _____

   adapt—to change in order to make something more suitable

   _____

   _____

Vocabulary: Meaning and Message © Fearon/Janus Publishers

Vocabulary Development: Confusing Words

Name _____ Date _____

2. **ascent**—the act of going up

_____

_____

assent—to agree

_____

_____

3. **expand**—to make or become larger

_____

_____

expend—to spend or use up

_____

_____

4. **pursue**—to follow

_____

_____

peruse—to read carefully

_____

_____

5. **disperse**—to scatter

_____

_____

disburse—to pay out

_____

_____

Vocabulary: Meaning and Message © Fearon/Janus Publishers

Puzzle

Name _____ Date _____

A. Read each clue. Write the letter on the line.

CLUES:

1. The first letter of this word is in *pan* but not in *tan*. _____

2. The second letter is in *bun* but not in *bin*. _____

3. The third letter is in *far* but not in *fat*. _____

4. The fourth letter is in *is* but not in *it*. _____

5. The fifth letter is in *rut* but not in *rat*. _____

6. The sixth letter is in *fare* but not in *far*. _____

Now solve the puzzle. Write the letters from above on the lines to complete this sentence.

___ ___ ___ ___ ___ ___ your dream.

B. Follow the same directions as above.

CLUES:

1. The first letter is in *get* but not in *got*. _____

2. The second letter is in *camp* but not in *cap*. _____

3. The third letter is in *less* but not in *loss*. _____

4. The fourth letter is in *tar* but not in *tap*. _____

5. The fifth letter is in *leg* but not in *less*. _____

6. The sixth letter is in *ten* but not in *ton*. _____

Write the letters from above on the lines to complete this sentence.

The truth will slowly ___ ___ ___ ___ ___ ___ .

Vocabulary: Meaning and Message © Fearon/Janus Publishers

Word Power: Conjunctions and Interjections

Name _____ Date _____

What is the difference between these two sentences?

> Jenny and I will be there.
> Jenny or I will be there.

The first sentence says that two people will be present, Jenny *and* I. The second sentence says that only one person will be present, either Jenny *or* I. The words that make these sentences different are called **conjunctions.** A conjunction is a word that joins words, groups of words, and sentences. Here are some more examples:

> Neither Michelle *nor* Toni is here.
> I ordered it, *so* I guess I'll have to pay for it.
> She looks happy, *yet* I wonder if she is.
> He leaped without looking, *for* he was scared.

A. Use each of these conjunctions in a short sentence.

1. **but** _____

2. **nor** _____

3. **so** _____

If you were to win a big prize, you might be left speechless. If you weren't, you might say something like, "Wow!" or "Hurray!" These words are called **interjections.** An interjection is a word that expresses strong emotion. Here are some more examples of interjections:

Ouch   Oh   Yuk   Eek   Gee   Ah
Oh, no   Ugh   Really   Well   Hey   Help

Interjections sometimes stand alone as separate sentences:

> Help! I'm drowning!

An interjection can also appear at the beginning of a sentence:

> Oh, no, I forgot my wallet!

As you can see from the sentences above, interjections should be followed by either and exclamation point or a comma.

B. Use each of these interjections in a sentence.

1. **Wow** _____

2. **Ouch** _____

3. **Oh, no** _____

Writing on Your Own

Name _____ Date _____

Suppose your school has just received some money for an after-school sports program. The school can now form teams and have practice sessions in four different sports. Which four sports would you recommend? Keep in mind that the sports program will be for all the students. Also remember that the money is limited. So you might not want to suggest sports that would cost a great deal of money. For example, building a pool for a swim team might be too costly. List your sports below. After each, tell why you chose that sport.

Sport #1 _____

_____

_____

_____

Sport #2 _____

_____

_____

_____

Sport #3 _____

_____

_____

_____

Sport #4 _____

_____

_____

_____

On a separate sheet of paper, write a short letter to the head of the sports department. Try to convince that person that your four sports are the best ones to have in the program. Explain your reasons. You might also explain why you feel certain other sports should *not* be included in the program.

Lesson 2, Exercise 7
Test

Name _____ Date _____

Choose the best word to complete each sentence.

1. The highway patrol arrived at the scene of the _____.

   A. collision   B. expend   C. elapse   D. ascent

2. You'll meet your goal if you _____ it with courage.

   A. emerge   B. pursue   C. ascent   D. disperse

3. An icy wind made the _____ up the mountain difficult.

   A. pursue   B. disperse   C. ascent   D. adept

4. This chef can prepare any meal. He is _____ in all cooking styles.

   A. ascent   B. angle   C. emerge   D. adept

5. The flagpole makes a 90-degree _____ with the ground.

   A. angle   B. disperse   C. expend   D. pursue

6. The general's troops were _____ across the field.

   A. angled   B. dispersed   C. ascent   D. expended

7. The basketball game's last quarter has nearly ended. Eleven minutes have already _____.

   A. elapsed   B. dispersed   C. pursued   D. expend

8. At season's end, the Nuggets _____ as the champs.

   A. emerged   B. dispersed   C. collision   D. adept

9. This job requires me to _____ much time and effort.

   A. incredible   B. pursue   C. adept   D. expend

10. No one expected this. It's just _____!

    A. collision   B. incredible   C. adept   D. angle

Reading on Your Own

Name _____ Date _____

As you read this story, think about the meaning of each highlighted word.

The New Kids

Do you know Joe, Donnie, Jordan, Danny, and Jon? If you follow popular music, you **probably** don't need to ask who they are. They're the New Kids on the Block. Their music has made them one of the most **prominent** groups on today's scene. They have fans all over the world.

The band was started in 1984 by a man named Maurice Starr. Starr, a record producer, had decided to put together a group. He began listening to young people who were playing music in the Boston area. Starr met with those he **admired** and talked with them. The first person he hired was Donnie Wahlberg. Donnie was only 15, but he was **quite** grown up for his age. Starr could see that Donnie was able to get in touch with those who heard him sing. Good **communication** with an audience is a **necessary** skill for a singer to have.

Donnie introduced Starr to Danny Wood. Donnie and Danny then brought in two brothers, Jordan and Jon Knight. Starr found the last band member when he met Joe McIntyre, who was only 13.

At first the group was named "Nynuk." Some of the boys weren't **satisfied** with that name. They didn't think it was appropriate for a rock band. One day, Starr wrote a song called "New Kids on the Block." Everyone realized this was the perfect name for the group.

In 1988, their breakthrough album *Hangin' Tough* led to appearances in concerts and on television. Soon after, the boys were **visible** everywhere. When fans began following their every move, they knew they had **definitely** achieved fame.

Today, New Kids albums sell millions of copies. This doesn't seem to have gone to the band members' heads, though. To the **extent** that they can, they lead normal lives. They just happen to be one of the busiest and best-loved groups in the world!

What question would you like to ask your favorite musician?

_____

_____

_____

Vocabulary: Meaning and Message © Fearon/Janus Publishers

Using Context

Name _____ Date _____

Choose words from the box to replace the highlighted words.

visible	necessary	admire	satisfied	prominent	
probably	communication	definitely	quite	extent	

1. Henry was **pleased** with the results.

   _____

2. To pass the test, it is **needed** that you study.

   _____

3. I am looking forward to it and will **certainly** be there.

   _____

4. A rainbow was **able to be seen** after the spring shower.

   _____

5. We all **think highly of** your talent.

   _____

6. The dinner Edna cooked was **rather** delicious!

   _____

7. The meeting was attended by **widely known** scientists.

   _____

8. I will **almost surely** be able to go.

   _____

9. I'll help to the **amount or limit** that I am able.

   _____

10. Our **exchange of ideas and feelings** was by letter.

    _____

Vocabulary Development: Prefixes

Name _____ Date _____

What do you do if you want to use a word whose meaning you want to change? How do you change the word? One way is to put a group of letters with the meaning you want in front of the word. This group of letters is known as a **prefix.**

For instance, look at the word *handle.* One of its meanings is "to deal with." You could say, "I can *handle* this problem. It's not too difficult." Now suppose you add the prefix *mis-* to the beginning of the word *handle.* You get a new word, *mishandle.* It means something very different from *handle.* The prefix *mis-* means "not" or "badly." To *mishandle* is to "handle badly." You might use this word to say something like, "The problem is so difficult that I'm afraid I'll mishandle it."

Here are some common prefixes and their meanings:

Prefix	Meaning	Sample Words
mis-	wrongly; badly; not	misread
im-, in-, ir-, un-	not	impolite; injustice; irreversible; unpleasant
inter-	among; between	interstate
re-	again; back	rethink
dis-	not or opposite; lack of	disinterest
anti-	against	antisocial
over-	over; excessive	overeat
bi-	having two; happening every two	bimonthly

Knowing what prefixes mean can greatly increase your vocabulary. For instance, suppose you come across the word *disinterest* in your reading. If you know the meanings of the word *interest* and the prefix *dis-,* you can guess that disinterest means "lack of interest."

A. Combine the prefixes with the words to make new words. Write the new words and use each one in a sentence. You may use a dictionary if you're not sure of word's meaning.

1. **in- + visible =** _____

   _____

2. **im- + probable =** _____

   _____

Vocabulary: Meaning and Message © Fearon/Janus Publishers

Vocabulary Development: Prefixes

Name _____ Date _____

3. in- + definitely = _____

_____

4. mis- + communication = _____

_____

5. un- + necessary = _____

_____

6. dis- + satisfied = _____

_____

7. over- + grown = _____

_____

B. Match each prefix in the box with one of the words listed
   below. If you're not sure you've made a real word, check in
   a dictionary. Write the new word and use it in a sentence.

re-   inter-   bi-   im-   over-

1. _____ + weekly = _____

_____

2. _____ + possible = _____

_____

3. _____ + take = _____

_____

4. _____ + read = _____

_____

5. _____ + city = _____

_____

Puzzle

Name _____ Date _____

The words in the box can be found in the puzzle below. They may be written in any direction. Find and circle each one. You may want to check off each word in the box after you have circled it. One word has been circled and checked as an example.

communication	extent	probably
quite	prominent	necessary	admire
satisfied	visible	✔definitely

```
c q r a d m i r e m q e
o w s d f g h l u p p o
m z c e b n r m e v e t
m y g t g o j l m g s t
u r u a p x b v r b d n
n a s i d i g e h j t e
i s v r s e e x t u f n
c s r i g t h t j k s i
a e v o i h j e i o g m
t c t u y u i n o p i o
i e q r q w z t a d e r
o n v p r o b a b l y p
n x s a t i s f i e d n
w e (d e f i n i t e l y)
```

Word Power: Unusual Comparisons

Name _____ Date _____

Suppose there are three children in your family. One would be *young*. Another would be *younger*. The third would be *youngest*. One of the children may work *carefully*. Another may work *more carefully* than that child. The third may work the *most carefully* of all.

These comparisons were formed by using the suffixes *-er* and *-est* and the words *more* and *most*. However, not all adjectives and adverbs form their comparisons in this way. Some have *irregular* comparisons. Note that the second sentence in each group of examples compares two things or actions. The third sentence compares three or more things or actions. Here are a few examples:

Roberto is a *good* guitar player.   I ran *far*.
Ted is a *better* guitar player.   Bill ran *farther*.
Joe is the *best* guitar player of all.   Wan ran *farthest*.

Gonzo is a *bad* dog.   Hester has a *little* clay.
Felix is a *worse* dog.   Marcus has *less* clay.
Spike is the *worst* dog of all.   Kathy has the *least* clay.

Ike sings *well*.   Sherry has *many* books to read.
Olivia sings *better*.   Abe has *more* books to read.
Pete sings *best* of all.   Conchata has the *most* books of all to read.

The comparative forms of adjectives and adverbs can be found in most dictionaries. They are usually listed after a word's part of speech.

Rewrite each sentence using the correct form of the highlighted word. Note whether two things or more are being compared.

1. That was the **worse** film I've seen in years.

   _____

   _____

2. Fu is the **better** singer in the school choir.

   _____

   _____

3. The moon is **far** from earth than I thought.

   _____

   _____

Lesson 3, Exercise 6
Writing on Your Own

Name _____ Date _____

Suppose you were to start your own musical group. What name would you give it? Why would you choose this name?

_____

_____

Which of your friends would you want to have in your group? Why?

_____

_____

What instruments would each of you play?

_____

_____

_____

What kind of music would you play?

_____

What do you think life would be like if your group were to become famous?

_____

_____

_____

_____

_____

_____

Vocabulary: Meaning and Message © Fearon/Janus Publishers

Test

Name _____ Date _____

Choose the best word to complete each sentence.

1. The house on the hill is _____ for miles.

   A. emerge   B. visible   C. necessary   D. extent

2. I can't help but _____ your courage.

   A. necessary   B. probably   C. quite   D. admire

3. Four _____ artists will decide which painting will win.

   A. extent   B. visible   C. quite   D. prominent

4. Between now and dinner, I will _____ get hungry.

   A. probably   B. quite   C. extent   D. prominently

5. I searched all over. Bill is _____ gone.

   A. communicate   B. extent   C. visible   D. definitely

6. When the phone lines fell, _____ was impossible.

   A. communication   B. visible   C. admire   D. extent

7. Food is _____ to life.

   A. quite   B. definitely   C. necessary   D. communicated

8. The full _____ of the damage is unknown.

   A. prominent   B. visibility   C. extent   D. quite

9. Rhonda was _____ with the results of her work.

   A. visible   B. satisfied   C. necessary   D. admire

10. The map you drew made the directions _____ clear.

    A. quite   B. visible   C. probably   D. extent

Reading on Your Own

Name _____ Date _____

As you read this story, think about the meaning of each highlighted word.

Singing on Stage

Have you ever seen a musical performed on a stage? Musicals are plays that have a lot of songs and usually dancing in them. In a good musical, the scenery and costumes are colorful, and the singing and dancing performances are very lively.

Many musicals are performed in a part of New York City called Broadway. A large number of the city's theaters are located there. However, the modern musical wasn't born on Broadway. Musicals began in Europe over 200 years ago. At that time, some writers felt that people shouldn't *say* words on stage but should *sing* them instead. So these writers **devised** stories in which the characters would sing about their feelings. Over the years, popular songs were **introduced** into the plays. Comedy was also added. Some people disapproved of the shows that weren't about serious subjects, but most people loved them because they were so entertaining.

One of the most popular recent musicals is called *Cats. Cats* is based on a group of poems by T. S. Eliot. In the show, the actors wear **costumes** that are often **bizarre.** The costumes have tails and whiskers that resemble those of real cats. The actors purr and meow and crawl all over the stage **pretending** to be cats. However, they sing as humans do. The cat characters have funny names, including Gumbie Cat and Grizabella. This **latter** character sings a beautiful song called "Memory." This song has become quite popular. Most audiences find *Cats* **altogether** enjoyable. In 1991, it had **already** been running on Broadway for nine years.

You may have the **occasion** to see a musical. Often these shows travel all over the country, from city to city. Some, such as *The Wiz, A Chorus Line, The Sound of Music,* and *Annie,* are made into movies. If you're really **interested** in musicals, however, try to see one on stage. Nothing beats the magic of a live performance.

If you were going to sing in front of an audience, what song would you sing? Why?

_____

_____

_____

Vocabulary: Meaning and Message © Fearon/Janus Publishers

Using Context

Name _____ Date _____

Circle the word that is being described.

1. clothing worn to make one look like a different person or like something else

   costume   devise   bizarre

2. by or before a certain time

   altogether   pretend   already

3. the one nearer to the end; the last one mentioned

   altogether   occasion   latter

4. to make believe

   pretend   occasion   latter

5. concerned; curious

   interested   pretending   altogether

6. to present one person to another; to bring into use; to start

   occasion   altogether   introduce

7. completely; in all; everything having been considered

   occasion   altogether   already

8. a way to do something; to think up

   altogether   occasion   devise

9. an opportunity; an important event; the time when something takes place

   bizarre   pretend   occasion

10. very odd or strange; peculiar

    costume   bizarre   latter

Vocabulary: Meaning and Message © Fearon/Janus Publishers

Lesson 4, Exercise 3
Vocabulary Development: Analogies

Name _____ Date _____

On page 98, you learned about analogies. As you recall, analogies show relationships between words. For example:

Finger is to *hand* as *nose* is to _____.

    a. breathe   b. nostril   c. face   d. blow

To solve an analogy question, first figure out the relationship between the first two words, *finger* and *hand*. A finger is part of a hand. Now, find the same relationship between nose and one of the four possible answers. Ask yourself, "What is a nose part of?" The answer is "face."

Circle the letter beside the word that completes the analogy.

1. **Bizarre** is to **strange** as **yell** is to _____.

    a. whisper   b. holler   c. mouth   d. weird

2. **Hurry** is to **rush** as **final** is to _____.

    a. first   b. race   c. prize   d. latter

3. **Hard** is to **soft** as **approve** is to _____.

    a. disapprove   b. devise   c. interest   d. smooth

4. **Pajamas** is to **sleep** as **costume** is to _____.

    a. dream   b. wear   c. Halloween   d. school

5. **Critic** is to **reviews** as **artist** is to _____.

    a. newspaper   b. paintings   c. movies   d. brushes

6. **Below** is to **beneath** as **event** is to _____.

    a. party   b. fancy   c. beyond   d. occasion

7. **Night** is to **day** as **huge** is to _____.

    a. tiny   b. large   c. wide   d. gigantic

8. **Drink** is to **milk** as **eat** is to _____.

    a. mouth   b. beverage   c. apple   d. hungry

9. **Create** is to **make** as **destroy** is to_____.

    a. build   b. building   c. ruin   d. art

Vocabulary: Meaning and Message © Fearon/Janus Publishers

Vocabulary Development: Analogies

Name _____ Date _____

10. **Awake** is to **asleep** as **grumpy** is to _____.

    a. dead   b. joyous   c. unhappy   d. ugly

11. **Baby** is to **child** as **warm** is to _____.

    a. hot   b. bath   c. freezing   d. crying

12. **Teacher** is to **classroom** as **judge** is to _____.

    a. criminal   b. court   c. verdict   d. jury

13. **Feet** is to **walking** as **wings** is to _____.

    a. angel   b. flying   c. falling   d. robin

14. **Sahara** is to **desert** as **Amazon** is to _____.

    a. dry   b. cold   c. hot   d. river

15. **Scotland** is to **country** as **Alabama** is to _____.

    a. state   b. city   c. planet   d. Mississippi

16. **Violin** is to **instrument** as **rose** is to _____.

    a. garden   b. flower   c. smell   d. water

17. **Odd** is to **unusual** as **dull** is to _____.

    a. boring   b. speech   c. exciting   d. train

18. **Instruct** is to **teach** as **honest** is to _____.

    a. cheat   b. hero   c. learn   d. trustworthy

19. **President** is to **Jefferson** as **athlete** is to _____.

    a. Cher   b. Dan Quayle   c. Michael Jordan   d. Hammer

20. **Child** is to **grown-up** as **seedling** is to _____.

    a. garden   b. plant   c. green   d. water

21. **Hotel** is to **room** as **zoo** is to _____.

    a. animals   b. cage   c. lion   d. bird

Puzzle

Name _____ Date _____

Unscramble the highlighted letters to form words from the box.

occasion	pretend	latter	interested	introduction
devise	costume	bizarre	already	altogether

1. Gregory wore a cowboy **s o m e c u t** on Halloween.
   _____

2. Seeing *The Sound of Music* was my **r o d i n t n i c u t o** to the theater. _____

3. Leila and Rose are my best friends. The former lives near me, but the **t a l e t r** lives in another state.
   _____

4. I saw many strange sights. The most **b a r e z i r** was a man dancing with a puppet that was as tall as he was.
   _____

5. My sister and I sometimes try to speak with British accents. We like to **t e n d e r p** we're from England.
   _____

6. I'm **t i n r e s t d e e** in your complaints.
   _____

7. I lost my keys and have to **s i d e v e** a way to get into the house without breaking any windows.
   _____

8. Tom was **g e t t o h e r a l** pleased with the party we gave him. _____

9. Ginger invited me to ride with her, but I had **l a d y a r e** made plans to ride with Sue. _____

10. His visit was a special **o n s o c c a i.**
    _____

Vocabulary: Meaning and Message © Fearon/Janus Publishers

Word Power: Noun or Verb?

Name _____ Date _____

Read these pairs of sentences. What do you notice about them?

> Can you *conduct* an orchestra?
> The Marine earned a medal for good *conduct*.

> Have you ever done a science *project*?
> Can you *project* your voice so that people in the
> last row of the theater can hear you?

In each pair of sentences above, one word is used as two different parts of speech. In the first example, the word *conduct* is used first as a verb meaning "to be in charge of," or "to direct." In the second sentence, *conduct* is used as a noun meaning "the way someone behaves." In each of these sentences, *conduct* is pronounced differently. As a verb, *conduct* is accented on the second syllable: con duct'. As a noun, *conduct* is accented on the first syllable: con' duct. Say the words aloud to hear the difference.

In the second pair of sentences, the word *project* is also used as two different parts of speech. In the first sentence, *project* is a noun meaning "an activity." In the second sentence, *project* is used as a verb meaning "to make one's voice heard." Again, pronunciation is different in each case. Can you pronounce each word correctly?

In a dictionary, the part of speech and the pronunciation of each word are given. If a word is used as more than one part of speech, separate definitions and pronunciations are given for each.

Look up each word in a dictionary. Then use the word in a sentence. Be sure to use the correct part of speech for each word.

1. **present**—noun _____

   _____

2. **present**—verb _____

   _____

3. **permit**—noun _____

   _____

4. **permit**—verb _____

   _____

Writing on Your Own

Name _____ Date _____

Have you ever wanted to perform before an audience? Explain.

_____

_____

_____

If you could be a performer, what kind of performer would you be? For example, you might want to be a movie star, a theater star, or a TV star. You might want to be a dancer, a singer, a musician, or a comedian. Explain your choice.

_____

_____

_____

Do you think you would get nervous before performing? Why?

_____

_____

_____

_____

If you could be one star who is already popular today, who would you choose to be? Why? What do you admire about this person or the life he or she leads?

_____

_____

_____

_____

_____

_____

Vocabulary: Meaning and Message © Fearon/Janus Publishers

Lesson 4, Exercise 7
Test

Name _____ Date _____

Choose the best word to complete each sentence.

1. I went to the museum, because I was _____ in dinosaurs.

   A. latter   B. pretending   C. interested   D. already

2. I prefer the _____ of the two.

   A. latter   B. bizarre   C. altogether   D. already

3. When the alarm went off, I was _____ awake.

   A. pretended   B. already   C. devised   D. latter

4. If I don't know the answer, I can't _____ that I do.

   A. devise   B. bizarre   C. costume   D. pretend

5. I don't know why I felt sad on what was supposed to have been a happy _____.

   A. altogether   B. costume   C. occasion   D. interested

6. Paul, I'd like to _____ you to Keesha.

   A. pretend   B. introduce   C. altogether   D. already

7. The old plan didn't work. We'll have to _____ a new one.

   A. devise   B. pretend   C. latter   D. occasion

8. Several party-goers wore the same _____.

   A. bizarre   B. costumes   C. occasion   D. altogether

9. It was an _____ boring party.

   A. interested   B. introduce   C. occasion   D. altogether

10. My brother is quite normal, but he wants us to think he's _____.

    A. occasion   B. bizarre   C. latter   D. interested

Unit 4 Review

Name _____ Date _____

A. Choose the word or phrase that means about the same as the highlighted word. Darken the circled letter.

1. kind **person**
   - Ⓐ listener
   - Ⓑ human
   - Ⓒ speaker
   - Ⓓ occasion

2. **speak** softly
   - Ⓐ pretend
   - Ⓑ ascent
   - Ⓒ expend
   - Ⓓ talk

3. **concede** victory
   - Ⓐ admit
   - Ⓑ disperse
   - Ⓒ elapse
   - Ⓓ satisfy

4. talk **together**
   - Ⓐ angle
   - Ⓑ with one another
   - Ⓒ elapse
   - Ⓓ adept

5. holiday **season**
   - Ⓐ time
   - Ⓑ angle
   - Ⓒ disperse
   - Ⓓ expend

6. train **collision**
   - Ⓐ crash
   - Ⓑ communication
   - Ⓒ necessary
   - Ⓓ extent

7. **satisfied** customer
   - Ⓐ private
   - Ⓑ random
   - Ⓒ admired
   - Ⓓ pleased

8. **necessary** change
   - Ⓐ prominent
   - Ⓑ needed
   - Ⓒ devise
   - Ⓓ admire

9. **pursue** one's dream
   - Ⓐ emerge
   - Ⓑ introduce
   - Ⓒ go after
   - Ⓓ elapse

10. **definitely** happy
    - Ⓐ probably
    - Ⓑ absolutely
    - Ⓒ difficult
    - Ⓓ already

11. **latter** date
    - Ⓐ second
    - Ⓑ pretend
    - Ⓒ satisfied
    - Ⓓ interested

12. **visible** from a distance
    - Ⓐ can be seen
    - Ⓑ bizarre
    - Ⓒ altogether
    - Ⓓ devised

13. **listen** to the teacher
    - Ⓐ occasion
    - Ⓑ disperse
    - Ⓒ admire
    - Ⓓ pay attention

Vocabulary: Meaning and Message © Fearon/Janus Publishers

Unit 4 Review

Name _____ Date _____

B. Darken the circled letter beside the word that is being described.

1. masks and clothing
   - (A) bizarre
   - (B) costume
   - (C) occasion
   - (D) pretend

2. most likely
   - (A) quite
   - (B) visibly
   - (C) definitely
   - (D) probably

3. the limit of something
   - (A) extent
   - (B) latter
   - (C) ascent
   - (D) expend

4. hard to believe
   - (A) necessary
   - (B) probable
   - (C) incredible
   - (D) visible

5. very much
   - (A) devised
   - (B) elapsed
   - (C) necessary
   - (D) quite

6. help
   - (A) guidance
   - (B) interested
   - (C) ascent
   - (D) emerge

7. set apart
   - (A) separate
   - (B) surprise
   - (C) speak
   - (D) already

8. make believe
   - (A) introduce
   - (B) communication
   - (C) pretend
   - (D) expend

9. strange
   - (A) occasion
   - (B) altogether
   - (C) bizarre
   - (D) interested

10. well-known
    - (A) necessary
    - (B) prominent
    - (C) bizarre
    - (D) ascent

11. event
    - (A) elapse
    - (B) track
    - (C) occasion
    - (D) guidance

12. respect
    - (A) admire
    - (B) emerge
    - (C) already
    - (D) pretend

13. skillful
    - (A) prominent
    - (B) listener
    - (C) adept
    - (D) separate

Glossary

A

add (ad) **verb, 1.** to find the sum of numbers **2.** to attach as something extra

a dept (ə dept′) **adjective,** masterful; expert

ad mire (ad mīr′) **verb,** to look at with approval

a gree (ə grē′) **verb, 1.** to share the same opinions or feelings **2.** to give consent **3.** to come to an understanding

a like (ə līk′) **adverb,** in a similar way; **adjective,** like one another

al ready (ôl red′ ē) **adverb,** by or before a certain time

al to geth er (ôl′ tə ge*th*′ ər) **adverb, 1.** completely **2.** in total **3.** on the whole

a mend ment (ə mend′ mənt) **noun,** a formal change made to a bill, law, or constitution

a mount (ə mount′) **noun, 1.** total; sum of two or more numbers **2.** a quantity; **verb, 1.** add up **2.** be equal in meaning or value

an ces tor (an′ ses tər) **noun,** any person from whom one is descended

an gle (ang′ gəl) **noun, 1.** the shape formed by two straight lines meeting at a point **2.** the space between or within those lines **3.** point of view about something; **verb,** to move or bend in an angle

a part ment (ə pärt′ mənt) **noun,** one or more rented rooms in which to live

ap pro pri ate (ə prō′ prē it *for adjective;* ə prō′ prē āt′ *for verb*) **adjective,** proper; correct; **verb,** to take for a particular use

ar e a code (âr′ ē ə kōd) **noun,** three numbers that are dialed when making a non-local telephone call

as cent (ə sent′) **noun, 1.** the act of going or climbing up **2.** an upward slope

as sis tance (ə sis′ təns) **noun, 1.** help given **2.** the act of helping

av er age (av′ ər ij *or* av′ rij) **noun, 1.** the number found by adding two or more numbers and then dividing by the number of numbers added **2.** the usual or normal amount or kind; **adjective, 1.** making up an average **2.** normal; ordinary; **verb,** to find an average

B

bal ance (bal′ əns) **noun, 1.** the amount left over **2.** the state in which two or more things or parts are of equal weight, amount, or value **3.** an instrument for weighing; **verb,** to make equal in weight or value

be tween (bi twēn′) **preposition, 1.** in or through the space or time that separates **2.** connecting **3.** involving

Bill of Rights (bil uv rīts) **noun,** the first ten amendments to the Constitution of the United States. It guarantees such rights as freedom of speech and of worship.

bill (bil) **noun, 1.** a statement of charges made and money owed **2.** a piece of paper money **3.** a poster or sign **4.** a draft of a law **5.** a bird's beak; **verb,** to make out a notice of money owed

bi zarre (bi zär′) **adjective,** strange; weird

bor row (bôr′ ō *or* bor′ ō) **verb,** to take something that will later be returned in order to use it for a while

C

cal cu late (kal′ kyə lāt′) **verb, 1.** to figure out a problem by using mathematics **2.** to estimate by examining the available information

cal en dar (kal′ ən dər) **noun, 1.** a chart showing the days, weeks, and months of the year **2.** a schedule of events

can cel (kan′ səl) **verb, 1.** to call off **2.** to cross out

cent (sent) **noun,** a coin used in the United States and Canada that is worth one hundredth of a dollar

cen tu ry (sen′ chə rē) **noun,** a period of one hundred years

change (chānj) **verb, 1.** to make or become different **2.** to exchange or substitute **3.** to put on other clothes; **noun, 1.** money returned when the amount given is more than the amount charged **2.** the act of making something different

cit y (sit′ ē) **noun,** a place where people live and work that is larger than a town

close (klōz *for noun and verb;* klōs *for adjective and adverb*) **noun,** end or finish; **verb, 1.** to shut **2.** to come to an end; **adjective, 1.** near **2.** careful **3.** almost equal

col lect (kə lekt′) **verb, 1.** to gather together **2.** to receive payment for

col li sion (kə lizh′ ən) **noun,** a crash

com mu ni ca tion (kə mū′ ni kā′ shən) **noun,** the act of sharing information, ideas, and feelings

con cede (kən sēd′) **verb, 1.** to admit or allow **2.** to admit defeat

con gress (kong′ gris) **noun, 1.** a meeting of people to discuss problems **2. Congress,** the branch of the United States government that makes laws and that includes the Senate and the House of Representatives

con sti tu tion (kon′ sti tü′ shən *or* kon′ sti tü′ shən) **noun, 1.** the laws on which the governments of states or countries are based **2. Constitution,** the laws on which the government of the United States is based

con tain (kən tān′) **verb, 1.** to hold **2.** to have inside or be made up of **3.** to hold back

cor rect (kə rekt′) **adjective, 1.** without any mistakes **2.** proper; **verb, 1.** to change to agree with certain standards **2.** to point out errors

cos tume (kos′ tüm *or* kos′ tūm) **noun,** clothing worn so that one looks like someone or something else

cul ture (kul′ chər) **noun,** the beliefs and customs of a society; its way of life

D

dan ger (dān′ jər) **noun, 1.** the likelihood that something bad may occur **2.** something that may cause harm

dec i mal (des′ ə məl) **adjective,** based on tens; **noun,** a fraction written with a point, such as: .5

def i nite ly (def′ ə nit lē) **adverb,** certainly, positively

del e gate (del′ i gāt′ *or* del′ i git *for noun;* del′ i gāt′ *for verb*) **noun,** a person appointed to speak for others; **verb,** to assign

de tail (di tāl′ *or* dē′ tāl) **noun,** any one of the small parts that make up a whole; **verb,** to describe thoroughly

de vise (di vīz′) **verb,** to think out or plan

dif fi cult (dif′ i kult′) **adjective, 1.** hard to do **2.** hard to get along with or please

dime (dīm) **noun,** a coin used in the United States and Canada which is worth ten cents

di rec to ry (di rek′ tə rē *or* dī rek′ tə rē) **noun,** a list of names and addresses, usually in alphabetical order

dis count (dis′ kount) **noun,** the amount taken off the usual price; **verb,** to subtract

dis perse (di spûrs′) **verb,** to scatter

dis tance (dis′ təns) **noun, 1.** the amount of space between two places or things **2.** a faraway place

du ty (dü′ tē *or* dū′ tē) **noun, 1.** that which a person is supposed to do **2.** tax paid on items brought in or out of a country

E

e con o my (i kon′ ə mē) **noun, 1.** the way a country, state, or household manages its money **2.** the efficient use of money

e lapse (i laps′) **verb,** to pass or slip by, said of time

e merge (i mûrj′) **verb, 1.** to come into sight **2.** to become known

e mer gen cy (i mûr′ jən sē) **noun,** a serious event that takes place without any warning and that requires immediate attention

em i grate (em′ i grāt′) **noun,** to leave one's own country to go to live in another place

en dorse (en dôrs′) **verb, 1.** to sign one's name on the back of a check **2.** to give approval to

en force (en fôrs′) **verb, 1.** to bring about by force **2.** to make sure that a rule or law is obeyed

en trance (en′ trəns *for noun;* en trans′ *for verb*) **noun, 1.** a place through which one enters **2.** the act of entering; **verb, 1.** to put into a trance **2.** to delight

en vi ron ment (en vī′ rən mənt *or* en vī′ ərn mənt) **noun, 1.** that which surrounds and which often includes such things as the air, water, and soil **2.** the conditions of a place

e qual (ē′ kwəl) **adjective, 1.** having the same size, value, or quality **2.** having the same rights

ex ec u tive (eg zek′ yə tiv) **adjective, 1.** having the power to decide, direct, or manage affairs in business and government **2.** referring to the presidency, the branch of the United States government that sees that laws are carried out; **noun,** a person who directs or manages

ex it (eg′ zit *or* ek′ sit) **noun, 1.** the way out **2.** the act of going out; **verb,** to leave

ex pend (ek spend′) **verb,** to spend or use up

at; āte; tär; shâre; end; wē; in; īce; fîerce; not; sō, lông; oil; our; up; ūse; trüe; pút; bûrn; chew; wing; shoe; both; mother; **hw** in **wh**ich; **zh** in trea**s**ure; **ə** in **a**bout, ag**e**nt, penc**i**l, c**o**llect, foc**u**s

ex port (ek spôrt′ *or* eks′ pôrt′ *for verb;* eks′ pôrt′ *for noun*) **verb,** to send items to another country for sale there; **noun,** an item that is sold to another country

ex tent (ek stent′) **noun,** the scope or range of something

F

fac to ry (fak′ tə rē) **noun,** a building or group of buildings where goods are manufactured

few (fū) **adjective,** not many; **noun,** a small number of people or things

fi nance (fi nans′ *or* fī′ nans) **noun, 1.** the management of money **2.** (plural) money or funds; **verb,** to supply the money for

fire es cape (fīr′ e skāp′) **noun,** an outdoor metal stairway used to get out of a building in the case of a fire

first aid (fûrst ād′) **noun,** emergency treatment given to a sick or injured person

for eign (fôr′ ən) **adjective, 1.** of or from a country other than one's own **2.** having to do with other countries **3.** unusual or strange

frac tion (frak′ shən) **noun, 1.** a part of a whole number, written in this form: $\frac{1}{2}$ **2.** a small part of something

free en ter prise (frē en′ tər prīz′) **noun,** an economic system in which business is carried out with limited government control

G

gen er a tion (jen′ ə rā′ shən) **noun, 1.** one stage in a family's history **2.** the average time between any two stages, usually considered to be about 30 years **3.** any group of people born at around the same time

gen tle man (jen′ təl mən) **noun, 1.** a well-mannered male **2.** a man of high social standing

group (grüp) **noun,** a number of persons or things put together or considered together; **verb,** to form into a group or groups

growth (grōth) **noun, 1.** the act of growing **2.** something that has grown

gui dance (gīd′ əns) **noun,** the act of supervising or advising

H

House of Rep re sen ta tives (hous uv rep′ ri zen′ tə tivz) **noun,** one of the two houses of the United States Congress

I

i den ti fy (ī den′ tə fī′) **verb, 1.** to point out or name **2.** to recognize

im mi grant (im′ i grənt) **noun,** one who comes to or who has come to live in a new country

in cred i ble (in kred′ ə bəl) **adjective, 1.** unbelievable **2.** amazing

in de pen dence (in′ di pen′ dəns) **noun,** free from the rule or control of others

in quire (in kwīr′) **verb,** to try to find out about something by asking questions

in ter est (in′ tər ist *or* in′ trist) **noun, 1.** a desire to know more **2.** a desire to take part in something **3.** advantage or benefit **4.** payment for the use of money; **verb, 1.** to cause to want to know more about something **2.** to cause to take part in

in tro duce (in trə düs *or* in trə dūs) **verb, 1.** to make acquainted with **2.** to bring (someone's) attention to

J

ju di ci ar y (jü dish′ ē er′ ē) **noun,** the branch of the United States government that interprets laws; the system of federal courts

K

knowl edge (nol′ ij) **noun, 1.** facts that are known **2.** that which is known **3.** the fact of knowing

L

lack (lak) **verb,** to need; to be without; **noun, 1.** the state of needing something **2.** that which is missing or is needed

la dy (lā′ dē) **noun, 1.** a well-mannered female **2.** a woman of high social standing

land lord (land′ lôrd) **noun,** a person or organization that rents out rooms, apartments, houses, buildings, or land to tenants

lat ter (lat′ ər) **adjective, 1.** the second mentioned of two **2.** coming near the end; **noun,** the second of two things mentioned

lease (lēs) **noun,** a written agreement allowing one to rent an apartment, a house, or land; **verb,** to rent

leave (lēv) **verb, 1.** to go away **2.** to quit **3.** to cause or allow to remain **4.** to deliver **5.** to hand over; **noun, 1.** permission to be absent from duty **2.** permission to do something

less (les) **adjective,** not as much; **adverb,** to a smaller degree or extent; **noun,** a smaller amount; **preposition,** minus

lim it (lim′ it)   **noun, 1.** a boundary **2.** the farthest point possible; **verb,** to restrict

lis ten er (lis′ ən ər)   **noun,** a person who tries to hear

loan (lōn)   **noun, 1.** the act of lending **2.** that which is lent; **verb,** to lend

M

man age (man′ ij)   **verb, 1.** to direct, control, or handle something **2.** to succeed at doing something

mass pro duc tion (mas prə duk′ shən)   **noun,** the production of goods in large quantities, usually with the help of machines and by a number of people working on one item, each doing a separate task

meas ure ment (mezh′ ər mənt)   **noun,** the act of finding the size, height, weight, and so on, of something

met ric (met′ rik)   **adjective,** having to do with the metric system, which is a system of measurement based on counting by tens

month (munth)   **noun,** one of the twelve divisions of the year, such as January or February

mort gage (môr′ gij)   **noun,** the giving of property as security for a loan

move ment (müv′ mənt)   **noun, 1.** the act of moving; motion **2.** the main part of a work of music **3.** the actions of a group of people taken to reach a goal **4.** a trend

N

nec es sar y (nes′ ə ser′ ē)   **adjective, 1.** needed or required **2.** unavoidable

nick el (nik′ əl)   **noun, 1.** a coin that is worth five cents **2.** a hard metal with a silver color

O

oc ca sion (ə kā′ zhən)   **noun, 1.** the particular time when something takes place **2.** a special event **3.** an opportunity

op er a tor (op′ ə rā′ tər)   **noun, 1.** a person who provides assistance or information about the phone system; **2.** a person who runs a machine or other device

op por tu ni ty (op′ ər tü′ ni tē or op′ ər tü′ ni tē)   **noun, 1.** a good chance **2.** the favorable or right time to do something

op pose (ə pōz′)   **verb, 1.** to be against **2.** to set against

out of or der (out uv ôr′ der)   **adjective,** not in working condition

own er (ō′ nər)   **noun,** the person who is in possession of something

P

peas ant (pez′ ənt)   **noun,** a person who lives in the country and works as a farmer or who owns a farm

per son (pûr′ sən)   **noun,** any man, woman, or child

pe ti tion (pi tish′ ən)   **noun,** a request, usually made formally, to a person in authority; **verb,** to make a formal request

po lice (pə lēs′)   **noun,** an organized group of people given the power to enforce laws and keep order; **verb, 1.** to control or protect **2.** to keep clean

pol lu tion (pə lü′ shən)   **noun,** the dirtying of the environment by harmful materials

pov er ty (pov′ ər tē)   **noun, 1.** the state of having little or no money **2.** lack

pre tend (pri tend′)   **verb,** to make believe

pri vate (prī′ vit)   **adjective, 1.** used by or belonging to individuals **2.** not seen or shared by others **3.** not holding a public office; **noun,** the lowest rank in the military

prob a bly (prob′ ə blē)   **adverb,** most likely

prom i nent (prom′ ə nənt)   **adjective, 1.** well-known or important **2.** easily visible because it stands out

prop er ty (prop′ ər tē)   **noun, 1.** anything that a person owns **2.** a piece of land **3.** an essential quality of something

pub lic (pub′ lik)   **adjective, 1.** of or for all the people in a place **2.** open to all the people **3.** working for the government of a place; **noun,** all the people of a particular place

pur sue (pər sü′ or pər sū′)   **verb, 1.** to go after in order to catch **2.** to carry out or follow

Q

quar ter (kwôr′ tər)   **noun, 1.** any of four equal parts **2.** a coin that is worth twenty-five cents **3.** one of four equal time periods into which certain games are broken up **4.** a district or section; **verb,** to divide into four equal parts

quite (kwīt)   **adverb, 1.** entirely or completely **2.** really or actually

R

real es tate (rēl′ e stāt′)   **noun,** land, along with the buildings, trees, and other things on it

at; āte; tär; shâre; end; wē; in; īce; fîerce; not; sō, lông; oil; our; up; ūse; trüe; pu̇t; bûrn; chew; wing; shoe; both; mother; hw in which; zh in treasure; ə in about, agent, pencil, collect, focus

re cy cle (rē sī′ kəl) **verb, 1.** to make something able to be used again **2.** to use again

reg is ter (rej′ ə stər) **noun, 1.** a machine used to add up and store money **2.** a formal listing of items **3.** the range of an instrument or a voice; **verb, 1.** to enter in a list or record **2.** to have one's name placed on a list **3.** to indicate

rent (rent) **noun,** payment made in return for the use of something; **verb, 1.** to get the right to use in return for payment **2.** to give the right to use in return for payment

res tau rant (res′ tər ənt *or* res′ tə ränt′) **noun,** a place where food is prepared and served

rest room (rest′ rüm *or* rest′ rüm) **noun,** a public washroom

S

sat is fy (sat′ is fī′) **verb, 1.** to meet a need or desire **2.** to convince

sea son (sē′ zən) **noun, 1.** one of the four divisions of the year: spring, summer, fall, and winter **2.** a time of year noted for its special activity; **verb,** to add spices and herbs to food

sen ate (sen′ it) **noun, 1.** the branch of a government that is in charge of making laws **2. Senate,** one of the two law-making branches of the United States Congress

sep a rate (sep′ ə rāt′, *for verb;* sep′ ər it *or* sep′ rit, *for adjective*) **verb,** to part; **adjective,** not joined

shelf (shelf) **noun,** a piece of wood or other material that is used to hold things and that is often attached to a wall

sign (sīn) **noun, 1.** something that points to or suggests something else **2.** a board or poster used to display information; **verb, 1.** to write one's signature on **2.** to communicate by using sign language

sin gle (sing′ gəl) **adjective, 1.** only one **2.** not married **3.** for one person; **noun,** a hit in baseball that allows the batter to get to first base; **verb, 1.** to pick out or choose from others **2.** in baseball, to hit a single

so ci e ty (sə sī′ i tē) **noun, 1.** all human beings, considered as a group **2.** a group of people joined by a common interest **3.** wealthy people **4.** a person's friends or associates

speak (spēk) **verb, 1.** to talk; to express ideas or feelings **2.** to make a speech

suc cess ful (sək ses′ fəl) **adjective,** having the result that was hoped for

su per in ten dent (sü′ pər in ten′ dənt) **noun,** a person in charge of directing or managing a department or building

sur prise (sər prīz′) **verb, 1.** to cause to feel wonder or amazement **2.** to come upon unexpectedly; **noun,** a feeling of wonder or astonishment

T

ten ant (ten′ ənt) **noun,** a person who pays rent to occupy rooms, an apartment, a house, a building, or land that belongs to someone else

to geth er (tə geth′ ər) **adverb, 1.** in union or contact with each other **2.** at the same time

track (trak) **noun,** a trail or a course for walking or running; **verb,** to follow

V

var y (vâr′ ē) **verb, 1.** to change in form **2.** to make or become different from another or others **3.** to be different

vis i ble (viz′ ə bəl) **adjective, 1.** able to be seen **2.** apparent

W

warn ing (wôr′ ning) **noun,** a notice that something bad might occur; **verb,** telling of danger

week (wēk) **noun,** a period of seven days

wil der ness (wil′ dər nis) **noun,** a large area in which no people live

with draw (with drô′ *or* with drô′) **verb, 1.** to take out **2.** to take back **3.** to go away